# HOW TO BE
# SWEDISH

A QUICK GUIDE TO SWEDISHNESS

IN 55 STEPS

–

MATTHIAS KAMANN

# MATTHIAS KAMANN

© Matthias Kamann, 2017

Publisher:
Matthias Kamann, Växjö, Sweden

Cover design and illustrations:
Matthias Kamann

1st edition, 2017

ISBN 978 91 983799 0 7

www.HowtobeSwedish.com

www.HejSweden.com

www.MatthiasKamann.com

*Dedication*

*To my parents, Margarete and Karl-Wilhelm, for their unconditional love and support.*

MATTHIAS KAMANN

# Introduction

"Vast forest, a lot of Volvos and blonde people everywhere," these were my first impressions after having arrived in the country in which I wanted to stay for a semester abroad. One semester turned into more than 10 years. And today, I call Sweden my new home country.

In this book I want to show you the quirks of the Swedish culture, so you can avoid the pitfalls and integrate into Swedish society without embarrassing yourself as much as I did.

This is the book I wish I had read before going to Sweden. It is a conclusion of what one learns after having spend more than a decade in this beautiful country.

You will find useful information for travelling, private and business interactions alike.

I hope you enjoy finding out "how to be Swedish"!

*Matthias Kamann*
January 2017, Växjö, Sweden

# Contents

# 1. Say "Hej"

*Hej* is the probably the first word you hear when you come to Sweden. The stewardess, the cashier at the gas station or the receptionist will most likely greet you with a very friendly and slightly high pitched *hej!*

Also, if you are in a good mood (or want to pretend you are), you can say a double: *hej, hej!*

The best way to learn how to correctly pronounce the Swedish word *hej*, is to go to a fashion or makeup store, where an over-ambitious young Swedish woman, in her forties, will most likely welcome you with a slightly exaggerated *hej, hejj!*

## How to Say "Good Bye" in Swedish

Swedes haven't come up with a proper *good bye* phrase, yet. They use *hejdå* when someone is leaving.

To say *good bye*, the laziest Swedes will just go for *hej* instead of *hejdå*. This is very common for highly efficient shop assistants. The benefit: when one customer is leaving and a new one steps into the store at the same time, the assistant has to say *hej* only once. Very smart.

## Ways to Greet a Swedish Person

Apart from *hej*, the following phrases and words can be applied depending on the depth of your relationship with a Swede.

- Formal: *God morgon/dag/kväll - Good morning/day/evening*
- Formal, person trying to be a little bit funny: *Goddagens - Good day/hello*
- Normal: *Hej - Hello*

- Alternative: *Hallå - Hello*
- Buddy-level: *Tjenare - Hi*
- Close buddy (or colleague who drinks a lot of beer): *Tja* (short form of *tjenare*) - *Yo*
- Buddy who wants to display his or her easygoing-ness whiel being fed up with saying *tjenare* or *tja* too often: *Tjabba - Yooo*

So, dear soon to be Swede, get used to saying *hej* many times a day. If you don't understand what Swedes say after that, just reply with a: *Jag pratar inte svenska. - I don't speak Swedish.* And then continue speaking English.

# 2. Have Many Coffee Breaks Called *Fika*

*Fika* is a big part of the Swedes' everyday life. Basically, *fika* just means *to have a coffee*. But it is so much more than just that. It has been described as a social institution or even phenomena. Swedish people - often portrayed as distant, calm and unsocial - love their *fika*. It gives them the opportunity to meet and hang out with friends, get to know new people, check out potential partners or network with business folks.

During leisure time, *fikas* tend to be a little longer than during work. From 30 minutes to several hours. The informality of a *fika* makes it easy for everyone to suggest or agree to meet for one.

*"Fika ['fiː₁ka]"*

## Fika at Work

At many work places, fika is part of the regular daily schedule. In the morning, a fika at 10:00 and in the afternoon at 15:00 is not uncommon.

For you *soon to be Swede* that means two extra breaks from work, lasting 10 to 30 minutes, called *fikarast* or *fikapaus*. When everyone else gathers in the meeting room, you'd better stop working and join the group. You won't get any extra points from your boss for pretending you have no time for a break, even if you claim your work is just too important to be paused.

Among the consensus-oriented Swedes, *fika* is a great way to exchange knowledge, opinions about what's going on in the company, and generally bond with your colleagues. This results in better productivity for the company and better well-being for each employee.

*"Swedes spend in total 9,5 days each year having fika."*

## What's on the Fika-Table?

Essential for a *fika* is the cup of coffee. But, of course, not everyone likes it. To have a tea, soda or any other drink instead is just as fine. Most Swedes combine their break with some pastry, called *fikabröd*. Among the most popular are *kanelbullar* (cinnamon buns), *chokladbollar* (chocolate balls) and biscuits.

## Where to Fika?

Preferably in a café or restaurant. Of course, you can also invite someone home for a fika. But preferably not for the first time you meet that person though, because that is perceived as an indirect invitation for getting cosy with each other.

If you don't feel like meeting up with someone, no problem, just go by yourself. Enjoy the atmosphere in the café and have a cup of good strong Swedish coffee.

## Fika History

The word *fika* originated from the 19th century word *kaffi* (coffee) - then Swedes switched the positions of the two syllables and removed one *f*.

*kaffi -> ffi-ka -> fika*

During the history of Sweden, coffee has been banned several times. Some Swedes didn't want to follow those rules, so they had to come up with a secret word when they wanted to arrange a meeting for having *kaffi*.

So, dear soon to be Swede, go have a fika! And, if you don't like the person you're meeting, or if you are getting bored, you can always say "Sorry, I have to go home now because I have booked a *tvättid*" (laundry time)'.

# 3. Be Obsessed with Summer and Sunshine

Winters in Sweden are long, dark and cold. These conditions have a severe effect on Swedish behavior. Swedes start longing for sunlight as soon as Winter arrives.

They leave home in the morning in darkness and come home in the evening in darkness. Then they spend the rest of the evening making vacation plans and fantasizing about warm, sunny summer days and drinking rosé wine outside in the nature, sitting on a *gräsmatta* (grass).

## Swedish Summer

> *"Summer is considered the most precious and beautiful week in Sweden."*

*Sommar* (Summer) only makes a short appearance in Sweden, especially in the north, and it usually doesn't last longer than maybe a few days in July. When a Swede tells you, "I had a romance that lasted all summer", it possibly wasn't more than just a one-night stand.

The seasons before and after summer are called *vår* (Spring) and *höst* (Autumn). But you won't hear these words too often in Sweden. Due to an even shorter appearance than summer, they play only a subordinate role in the Swedish weather consciousness.

During summer time, once the clouds disappear, Swedes take any opportunity to take a break from work, go out and sit down on the smallest pieces of *gräsmatta*, between the office building and car park. With a coffee to go or green smoothie in their hand, Swedes enter a meditative state, praising the sun for delivering warmth and refuelling the body with vitamin D. For Swedes, having a sunbath as soon as the sun is shining is very common, even if the temperatures are still around 5°C/41°F.

*"When Swedes pick their clothes for the day, they don't consider the outside temperature, but rather whether the sun is shining or not."*

Important to know: If you want to invite your Swedish friends on a sunny summer day, be aware that Swedes will reject any suggested leisure time activities that don't take place outdoors.

In restaurants and cafés, umbrella heaters and blankets help to keep Swedes warm and roasted when they *äter glass i solen* (eat ice cream in the sun), have a lunchtime coffee or weekend wine.

*"Sunny weather has a welcoming effect on Swedes. They suddenly start to talk while socializing."*

## Lobster Swedes

As soon as summer begins, Swedes start competing against each other. Who's going to be the one with the best tan, either in the office or among friends? Walking around in Sweden with red, sunburnt skin, is not considered a sign of stupidity, but rather a strong commitment to reaching the highest possible levels of sun intake.

So, dear soon to be Swede, adjust to this sunlight obsessive behavior and expose as much skin to the sun as legally possible!

# 4. Take off your shoes

You have come to Sweden and been invited over to a Swede's home. You are a bit nervous because you're not used to Swedish culture and customs yet. You ring the doorbell and your Swedish friend opens the door for you. You say '*Hej!*', your friend replies '*Nämen, hejjj! Välkommen in!*'

What do you do once you have stepped over the massive door sill onto a door mat? Right. You take off your shoes. Then you place them carefully in front of your friend's vast shoe collection which is usually sorted in a practical two level *sko hylla*, shoe rack.

If you're not used to taking off your shoes at home, make sure you don't embarrass yourself with socks that not only look like Swiss cheese but maybe even smell like it.

## Swedish Socks

Always wear a pair of fresh, immaculate socks. Some Swedes want to show their fashion sense of humor by wearing socks that are red, light blue, acid green or a striped combination of those colors. You should play the safe card here, choose black, and don't gamble with eye-exhausting color combinations.

## Fine Dress and Suit - but No Shoes

Now, imagine you're invited to a dinner with your friends, dress code: formal. Do you think you could keep on your freshly polished, shiny leather shoes or your favorite high heels at the party? Of course not. You're in Sweden. Everyone has to leave their shoes at the entrance and expose their feet to everyone's eyes - and often even to a cold floor.

You might think, but what if I brought a pair of my own house shoes? Sure! Go ahead! This is not considered strange in Sweden at all. I actually have a pair stored in the trunk of my car, just in case.

## Slippers on pre-parties

You should probably not consider bringing a pair of slipper house shoes to pre-party with students though. That could be a little embarrassing.

However, you might wish you had chosen slipper embarrassment over discomfort once you have stepped into a beer spill.

So, dear soon to be Swede: *Ta av dig skorna!* Take off your shoes!

# 5. Avoid Your Neighbors

You have moved into a Swedish apartment. Now, just like every other Swede, once in a while, you have to leave it, because you have to go to work or spinning classes or to the grocery store to buy *laktosfri mellanmjölk*, (lactose free "in between" milk).

Leaving your apartment, dear soon to be Swede, can put you into a tricky situation. To get to your bike or Volvo estate car, you first have to pass through the hallway of your apartment building. This is considered a danger zone. Why? Because you could bump into one of your neighbors. And you don't want to meet them because they might potentially attack you with *small talk*.

## Tjeeena!

Just like any other "real Swede", you should avoid *small talk* at all cost. You don't want to waste your precious time engaging in dull conversations, reporting about current weather conditions: *Tjeeena! Vilket fint väder idag!* (Hiii! What a nice weather today!)

Before you step out into the hallway, first listen carefully or look through your *titthål* (yes, a *door spy* really is called that way in Swedish), and see if a neighbor is currently patrolling outside your door. If you hear steps outside, don't go out yet! Just wait a few seconds!

To make your waiting time feel less awkward, check for a second time whether you have all your keys, wallet and mobile phone with you. Then, if no one is outside, get out and quickly lock the door.

If, however, you unexpectedly meet a neighbor who is on the way to his apartment, you can prevent further interaction: Say a short *Hej!* and try to avoid any eye contact.

Once you're outside the house, you're free!

So, dear soon to be Swede, get used to looking more often through your door-spy than into the eyes of your neighbors!

# 6. Avoid the Moose

Sweden is a large country. When you drive longer distances on a Swedish highway, you will notice high fences along most of the big roads. Those fences are not only there to prevent wild hunters from unexpectedly crossing the street but also to keep moose from taking a free ride on the bonnet of your car.

## Moose Safari

Sweden has the highest density of moose per square meter in the world. Not a surprise then that Swedes try to avoid any encounter with their national animal. Swedes just don't love moose as much as German tourists do.

For those tourists with no luck bumping into an *älg* on open roads, Swedes created *Moose Safaris* to satisfy the tourists' needs for taking pictures of these horny animals in a protected environment. It's a bit like the Swedish version of Jurassic Park, except the main attraction is walking around both inside and outside the fences and in the end, the visitors get the chance to eat the meat of the moose and not the other way around.

## Dangerous Moose

Crashing into a moose is life threatening. Due to their height and weight they can cause serious damage to cars and their passengers. It's recommended to drive around a moose instead of trying to go right through it.

The moose is the biggest land animal in Europe, alongside the polar bear. Also, if you go for a walk in the wild and see a moose, keep a safe distance! Although they are usually a bit shy, they might attack you in order to protect their little calves.

## Moose Hunt

There are about 300,000 moose in Sweden - until autumn. Since moose are very reproductive, Swedes organize a yearly *älgjakt,* moose hunt. About 50% of the *älg*-population is then shot, which is a lot compared to the (personally) estimated 0,0037% of all Swedish hunters being shot during hunting season.

## Drunk Moose

Moose have almost the same desire for alcohol as the Swedes. Since moose are not welcome in Swedish bars and nightclubs, their only option to get drunk is by eating fermented apples. Regularly in autumns, news magazines report about firemen who have had to remove a moose that got stuck its horns in an apple tree.

So, dear soon to be Swede, avoid the moose, at least on the same side of the fence!

# 7. Speak Swedish

Not many people in the world speak Swedish in their daily lives. Well, actually only the Swedes and a few Finns do. In total, about 10 million people.

## The Swedish Language

For many foreigners the Swedish language sounds rather pleasant, as if someone is singing, like a bird, on sunny spring day. It's very melodic and, unless you talk to Swedes from *Skåne* in the very south of Sweden, almost free of unpleasant [x] ch-sounds, (which you find plentiful in the Dutch language, for example).

## Easy to Learn

If you already speak English, then Swedish isn't the most difficult language to learn. The grammar is rather simple once you understand that there is no way to understand whether the article of a noun is *en* or *ett*. (In 80% of the cases, you are right saying it's *en* though.)

Apart from that, you'll be fine understanding the language after a short period, say a year. Speaking it fluently takes a bit longer. And if you are from a country with a less melodic language, adjusting to those *Swedish singing sounds* can get a little tricky.

Although I have been living in Sweden for many years, old-Swedes immediately point out that I'm originally German whenever I say: "*Jag gillar älgar och Drottning Silvia*", (*I like moose and Queen Silvia.*)

# Expressions and Weird Swedish Words

- *Läderlappen - Batman*
- *farthinder - speed bump*
- *fackförening - (trade) union*
- *bra* - No, not a part of the female wardrobe, it simply means *good*
- *knullruffs* - messy hair after intercourse
- *olla* - to touch something with one's glans (tip of the penis) - Yeah, isn't it super weird that Swedes have come up with a word for that!?

# Speak English, Very Well

If this is all too much for you and you'd rather want these words to never came out of your mouth, you can easily survive in Sweden without ever talking Swedish at all. Of course, integration in Sweden is much easier understanding and communicating with Swedes in their mother tongue, but you can actually get along rather well with just English.

About 90% of all Swedes speak English. Not just a little, you might be surprised how good they are. Just go to any café, order a Cappuccino in English and every waiter will reply to you in English without hesitating. Not just that, they will *not* roll their eyes when you don't try to speak the local language, which might happen in other countries in Europe; you know which I'm talking about...

# Compliments About English Skills

When Swedes are told their English is very good, they usually reply by saying that they've watched many English movies and TV programs, in their original language, but with Swedish subtitles. Therefore, they have been exposed to the English language from an early age.

So, on your way to Swedishness, try to speak Swedish, or at least some *Swenglish*!

# 8.  Look for the Ticket Dispenser

Swedes like it when things are tidy and well organized. They are also convinced that no one should take advantage of someone else. You can observe both traits combined when you watch them waiting in line.

## Queuing in Sweden

Whenever you enter a store, look for the number dispenser! If you miss it, things can go wrong...

For example, you've entered a place where the customers get counter service, like at the car-workshop, hospital, police station, pharmacy or even bank. You step ahead to the service desk while a friendly Swedish staff member says *hej* to a previous customer and pushes a button under the desk. You hear a buzzing noise and notice a display on the wall, two figures in red, showing a two-digit number, say 38. You suddenly understand; you've just passed a *nummerlapp-automat*.

You turn around and see the ticket dispenser close to the entrance door. Just as you decide to walk back to get your ticket, a new - much more informed - customer comes in and pulls a ticket. The ticket with the number 38, the one you missed. The person recognizes your desperation when you pull the 39 right after him and totally understands your mistake but pretends not to. Instead, he walks straight to the desk and orders a battery for his wrist watch.

## Calm Swedes

Even when they have to wait in line for a long time, Swedes don't moan or complain. They even keep their mouth shut and eyebrows down when a slow sales assistant is desperately trying to find out how to process a payment with a non-Swedish credit card.

So, dear soon to be Swede, next time you enter a Swedish pharmacy or bank, get your ticket from the ticket dispenser right away, and start staring at the digital display!

# 9. Own an *Osthyvel*

You have arrived in Sweden, bought a comfy bed, nice curtains, a table made of oak and timeless cutlery. A Swedish friend is over for a visit. You ask she is hungry and wants something to eat. If your guest is indeed hungry and a close friend, she might ask for something small, maybe "*en ostmacka, tack*", which means she wants a slice of bread with cheese.

As you are still an inexperienced soon to be Swede, you put the bread, butter and a piece of cheese on the table, next to a knife, a normal knife. Now your Swedish friend is completely confused, and wondering, "How the hell am I supposed to slice cheese without a proper *osthyvel*?" (cheese slicer). Of course your Swedish guest would never say these offending words, as Swedes avoid conflict at all cost. Instead she kindly asks if you, by chance, could give her "*en osthyvel kanske?*" (a cheese slicer, maybe?)

A Swedish kitchen is not complete without an *osthyvel*! So go and buy one, even if you don't eat cheese. Owning one makes you feel just that little more Swedish.

## Do you really need a cheese slicer?

Of course you don't *have to* use one to slice your cheese before carefully arranging the slices on your *knäckebröd*, (hard bread). Actually, if your coordination skills aren't too well developed, it might be a good idea not to put the inner side of your left thumb in danger. Imagine you put a little too much pressure while slicing, slip, and ... ouch!

But since you want to be more Swedish, put some effort and practice into it and next time a Swede dines with you, you can show off how Swedish you have become.

Be Swedish! Learn how to slice cheese with an *osthyvel*, without ending up in hospital.

So, dear soon to be Swede, buy an *osthyvel* and start puzzling your cheese slices on your *ostmackor* (cheese sandwiches)!

# 10. Drink Tap Water

You're sitting on a stylish chair in a fancy restaurant or standing in the middle of a fully packed dance floor. You feel an itch in your throat. The unpleasant feeling of thirst has taken over your body and mind. What do you do? You order *ett glas vatten, tack*!

Swedes have a close relationship to nature. So why not quench your thirst with the drink that comes directly out of it?

Many Swedes in the countryside even have their own well that supplies them with this liquid. This *vital liquid*, water, should not be confused with *Aquavit*! *Aquavit* literally means "*Life-Water*". But even though some Swedes might disagree, "*Akvavit*" is not really *vitally important*.

## No Need for Water in Bottles

Water fresh from the tap is of very high quality in Sweden. According to many Swedes, buying bottled water is pure waste, unless you like to observe rising bubbles. But even then, Swedes will just tell you to *get yourself a SodaStream®*.

Why carry heavy crates of bottled water and spend unnecessary time and money, if all you have to do is go to the kitchen and lift a little handle for a few seconds to quench your thirst?

## Free Water in Restaurants, Pubs and Clubs

Just take as much as you want. You get refreshing water everywhere and you don't need to feel embarrassed if you order a glass of tap water in a nice restaurant. They will bring you a glass or bottle, maybe even with ice an the slice of a lemon. But you definitely won't have to pay for it.

Another advantage: When you are partying in a club and notice that you - or one of your thirsty friends - have been drinking too much, you can cheaply avoid a potential vomiting disaster. Just say to the person behind the bar: *Min kompis behöver ett glas vatten!* - My friend needs a glass of water! It won't cost you anything and the staff won't be annoyed with you either.

So, dear soon to be Swede, enjoy a glass of fresh water from the tap, without concern!

# 11. Have Mixed Feelings about the Royal Family

Sweden has been a *constitutional parliamentarian monarchy* since, well, a very long time. Which means there is a constitution, a parliament, elected by the Swedes, and a king.

## King of Sweden

The official head of state is *King Carl XVI Gustaf* ('Carl Gustaf the sixteenth', or in Swedish *'Carl den sextonde Gustaf'*). Every four years, he inaugurates the newly elected parliament. A parliament that he otherwise has no influence on. He has no political power whatsoever. Actually even less power than a normal Swede, since he is neither allowed to express his political opinion publicly nor given the right to vote. At least he gets compensated, when each year, on the 10th of December, he may join a glamorous dinner to hang out with some of the world's smartest people and give them a nice prize, called the *Nobel prize* - you might have heard of it before.

## Discuss the Royal Family

Sweden is a country full of equality-minded people. Everyone gets a fair share of the fruits which Swedish society has planted over the past centuries. Most of what's received will be paid back in the form of high taxes, but that's something I'll discuss in a later chapter.

You, as a soon to be Swede, ambivalently should start liking the royal family while at the same time being sceptical about any system that enables someone to inherit wealth, power and privileges in any way. In conversations you should be able to state in one sentence *"how outdated the monarchy is"*, and in the next that you think *"crown princess Victoria will make an excellent queen."*

## 'Dela ut Pris och Klippa Band'

When talking about the main duties of the Swedish royal family, you or one of your Swedish conversation partners will say a sentence that contains the following words: *'dela ut pris och klippa band'*, basically meaning *'awarding prizes and joining ribbon cutting ceremonies'*. If your Swedish buddy hasn't said that sentence after three minutes, it's up to you to do so.

## Quick Lesson in Swedish Royal History

Back in the early 19th century, Sweden ran out of kings and queens. Which is why powerful Swedes decided to do a king-casting. Because back then, cultural imports from France were very much en vogue, they headhunted a former officer of Napoleon's crew, a guy called *Jean Bernadotte*. This explains why until today the Swedish royal family doesn't carry a more typical Swedish last name, like Johansson or Löfgrenqvistberg or something like that. Bernadotte sounds more fancy than Nilsson, doesn't it?

So, to become more like a Swede, join the appreciation and discussion about the royal family!

# 12. Love Swedish Nature

Swedes enjoy spending their time outside. They love being in touch with the beautiful Swedish nature.

But let's start with some basic facts about nature in Sweden...

## Facts About Swedish Nature

- More than half of the country is forest.
- Sweden has 95,700 lakes larger than 2 acres. That's a lot. And a good reason why Sweden is so attractive for mosquitos and Germans.
- There are 30,000 Swedish islands. But the only two you need to know are Öland and Gotland, both in the Baltic Sea, which is close to Russia.
- Sweden has a long coastline (7000 km/4350 miles).
- Swedes often have nature related names: first names such as *Björn* (bear), or surnames like *Åslund* (little forest on a ridge) or *Blomqvist* (flower twig).
- The Swedish national anthem describes the beautiful nature of Sweden, which is described as "*to die for*".
- Swedes are highly skilled about identifying flowers, toxic mushrooms, animals and all kinds of insects that you don't want to share your sleeping bag with.
- When you go to a Swedish doctor, because you suffer from stress or even anxiety, the advice he or she will give you is very likely: '*Go out for a walk and enjoy nature!*'.

## Beautiful Nature

In Sweden, to go out for a walk to find some relaxation is actually not a bad idea. Swedish nature indeed is beautiful. And it will certainly have a calming effect on your stressed soul.

You will probably fall in love with the idyllic lakes surrounded by forests; archipelagos with their softly shaped stone-islands rising from the water surface and little cottages, painted in red, embedded in a vast green landscape. Ideal for everyone who wants to be by oneself, once in a while.

No wonder that Swedes spend so much time outside in the nature, hiking, fishing, hunting, camping or going by boat.

## How to Win any Discussion with a Swede

When you have a serious discussion with Swedes (you probably won't notice that you're having one, because it'll feel like an ordinary conversation for you), just ensure to mention that your point of view is better for the environment and the Swedes will have to agree with you.

*"In Sweden, everything is good, as long as it's good for the environment."*

## Dangerous Animals in Sweden

Now that I've hopefully convinced you to spend some time in Sweden's nature, you'll probably ask yourself: are there any dangerous Swedish animals that I should be afraid of - like bears and wolves?

The answer is **yes**. There are bears and wolves. But don't worry. You're (rather) safe. They won't eat you unless you try to cuddle with their little babies.

So, dear soon to be Swede, go out more often and get in touch with the beauty of Sweden's nature!

# 13. Don't Work in July

Why work when no one else does?!

During the month of July, almost all Sweden go on holiday. Some stores are closed, so are a few hospitals - no reason for Swedes to get ill when the sun is shining. And even some police stations shut down entirely; no crime to solve when criminals are on vacation as well.

## Summer Jobs

Don't work in July, unless you're under 25 years old. Then you may have a summer job to replace all the sun-seeking holiday-Swedes. This means, during July, basically all of Sweden is run by teens and tweens.

## Country Defence

Swedes haven't been at war for over 200 years.
Why didn't they? Maybe because someone has told them that they also would have to fight during the month of July as well. *Inte okej* for Swedes.

They consistently decline any offer to attend wars, because they know these battles would interfere with their plans to travel to Thailand or precious weeks in their *sommarstuga* (summer cottage).

*"If any country ever contemplates invading Sweden, they surely will do it during the month of July."*

So, do like all Swedes with a full time job do, stay out of the office, all July!

# 14. Dress Like a Swede

Undoubtedly, Swedes have a good sense of fashion. Many centuries ago, Swedes expressed their personality wearing fur, leather and - legend says it - funny helmets with horns. Since then, a few things have changed in Swedish wardrobes.

*"Within a few centuries only, Swedes turned from wild looking Vikings into sidewalk-fashion-queens."*

Now, take a look in the mirror. That's how you look. Looks just fine, right?! Then look at a picture of a Swede and you will notice that they look a little bit different. Regardless of your nationality, there is a high probability that the Swede is bit better dressed than you, and has a slightly fresher, and more modern haircut.

To look like a Swede, you should cleanse your closet and start dressing fashionably. *Fashionably* in Sweden pretty much means wearing something similar or rather the same clothes that your Swedish friends wear.

Since all Swedes pretend to be friends, everyone wears items that practically look the same.

## Must-have Clothes in Sweden

Girls must furnish their wardrobe with: a black leather jacket, big scarf, tight black jeans and a pair of white Converse.

Guys on the other hand should own: black leather jacket, big scarf, tight black jeans and a pair of white Converse.

## Swedish Hairstyle

Swedes not only dress well, but they also make sure they look good on and around their head. Women, whose hair color is neither on the blond nor the dark side of the scale, might find themselves in a bit of a dilemma. To get rid of their, as Swedes call it, *råttfärg* (rat-color), they have to decide whether they dye their hair dark or blond.

## Black is the New Black

> *"The range of colors in a Swedish wardrobe is as diverse as a Swede's range of facial expressions."*

The only colors you are allowed to wear during the winter season are black and white - this is because Swedes seem to strictly stick to the "no-fun-colors during no-fun-times"-rule. If you want to see a Swede wearing something colorful in winter, you'd have to go to the gym or a sports event.

## Fashion inspiration

You don't know what to wear in Sweden? Get some inspiration by watching people on *Biblioteksgatan*, a shopping street in Stockholm. There, flagship stores of big Swedish and international brands are lined up. And so are the fashion conscious customers, passing by the cafés, showing off their latest purchases and branded shopping bags. Looking *stiligt* (stylish).

So, dear soon to be Swede, now that you have some insight into the Swedish fashion taste, go put on your minimalist black dresses and white sneakers!

# 15. Quit Smoking, Have *Snus* Instead

Many people in countries from all over the world have addictions. Most of them are legal. Some, for example, eat smelly cheese (French) and others smoke marihuana (looking at you Dutchies).  Swedes, on the other hand, are addicted to something else...

*Snus: the Swedes' favorite addiction - apart from coffee*

You might have noticed that some Swedes carry along a little round container in their pockets. It is roughly the size of an ice hockey puck or candy tin. What it contains is nothing sweet, but for many Swedes, something that's just as desirable as candy: *snus.*

*Snus is Swedish for 'snuff' or 'smokeless tobacco'.*

Swedes either put the tobacco loosely portioned in the mouth or they insert small white pillows which look like tiny tea-bags.

## Snus Privileges in Sweden

Snus is actually forbidden to be sold in most EU-countries, but Sweden successfully received some extra selling-privileges due to heavy lobbying in Brussels.

The Swedish top snus lobbyist (probably) said: "If we stop selling snus in Sweden, people will start to smoke more. Therefore, they have to go out in the cold. Therefore, they have to leave their desks during working hours. Therefore, we lose 1 billion Swedish crowns GNP per year. The exact 1 billion we'll request from the EU in subsidies. Do you EU-parliamentarians really want that?!" Problem solved. Snus sales legalized.

## Snus Consumption

Roughly one in four Swedish men consume snus regularly. In average 3.5 tins per week. It's more common than smoking, which about 14% of the Swedish people shorten their life-expectancy with.

## Snus Talking

It's totally common that a Swede - in the middle of a conversation - puts his or her index finger into their mouth to remove a snus-bag and either puts it back in the tin's extra compartment for used *snus-pillows* or just drops it on the street. The latter disposal option is not recommended though.

Snus is also the reason why many Swedes talk a bit weird. A snus-bag prevents the upper lip from moving freely. A good excuse for Swedes to speak even less than they already usually do.

## Advantages of Snus

To round things up, being addicted to snus has a few advantages (over being a smoker)
- You don't disturb the people around you as much.
- Your lounges are less affected, which is probably great if you have asthma.
- You can get your regular nicotine-dose while being inside.

## Disadvantages

- Teeth turning yellow/brown.
- Your teethridge is harmed.
- Funny facial expressions and mumbling sound while talking.

So, if you want to follow your nicotine addiction like a Swede, do it with snus instead of smoking!

# 16. Have Three Goals in Life: Villa, Volvo, Vuvve

Swedes are humble people. They don't show off. Or, if they do, they do it in a subtle way. Even the rich and successful Swedes, like for example the members of ABBA, are approachable and rarely try display their financial power through material possessions.

## Swedish Goals in lLife

In Sweden, people don't strive to become the richest or best at something. They are happy with just a few things.

As a proper Swede, your main goals in life should be: Villa, Volvo, Vuvve (literally: house, Volvo, dog).

## Goal #1: Villa

Let's start with the house. It doesn't have to be a big house. A small, wooden one already does the job. Those houses can be cheap in Sweden, depending on the location, of course. You can buy one for 50,000 Euros, somewhere a bit further away from a bigger city, in the forest.

## Goal #2: Volvo

To accelerate the integration process in Sweden, good advice would be to drive a Volvo. To decrease integration speed, particularly in conversations about cars, you should mention that Volvo nowadays is owned by a Chinese company. Swedes try not to think about that too much. They rather want their car brands to be purely Swedish - just as Swedish as the very popular Volvo-ambassador, Zlatan.

*"Volvos are considered reasonable cars: appealing looks, solid, safety-oriented, not showing off too much. Just like a typical Swede."*

Swedes consider Volvo as the safe choice. 20% of all cars on Swedish roads carry the badge with the male symbol on the bonnet. No one can turn up one's nose when you tell them you drive a Volvo V70 or V90. It's the car everyone can drive - it's classless in Sweden. Teachers, plumbers, architects and royals alike.

If you drive a Volvo in Sweden, you'll never have to explain why you made this choice over another car.

Now, if you really don't want to drive a Volvo, show some respect to the taste of Swedes, at least get a *kombi* (estate wagon) from another manufacturer.

# Goal #3: Vuvve

Get a proper dog. Preferably one that cats won't laugh about.
The top three most popular dogs in Sweden are:
1. Labrador retriever
2. Schäfer (German Shepherd)
3. Golden retriever

You should also consider giving your dog a typical Swedish dog name. The most popular names for dogs in Sweden: *Molly* for her and *Ludde* for him.

# Villa Volvo Vuvve

Now, dear soon to be Swede, once you've checked all the boxes of your 'life-goal-to-do-list', you can put your Ludde or Molly in the trunk of your Volvo estate car or play with him or her in the backyard of your Swedish house! Achieving this will give you a huge step ahead towards accomplished Swedishness.

# 17. Understand Swedish Beer Classification

Swedes not only drink vodka or *filmjölk*. Here and there, they also like to have a bottle of beer. Preferably from a Swedish brand.

Since Swedes are very alcohol conscious, they came up with three different classifications of beer, sorted by the contained percentage of alcohol. Less alcohol, means beer connoisseurs can drink more beer without getting too drunk too quickly. Or, to say it with the words of a Swede, '*You know which beer to drink to get drunk faster*'.

You should know about these classifications, because you don't want to show up at a pre-party inviting your friends for a can of *lättöl* (light beer). It's time to have a closer look at the labels on Swedish beer bottles.

## Beer Classification in Sweden

Beer is divided into three classes in Sweden. These classes also determine age restrictions for purchases.

## Class I

* *Lättöl* (Light beer) <2.25%

## Class II

* *Lätt Folköl* (Light People's Beer) <2.8%
* *Folköl* (People's Beer) <3.6%

For both classes, I and II, the buyer must be at least 18 years old.

## Class III

- *Mellanöl* (In-between beer) 3.6% - 4.5%
- *Starköl* (Strong beer) >4.5%

Class III may be sold to people aged 20 or above in state-owned alcohol shops *Systembolaget,* or in pubs to people aged 18 or above.

**LÄTTÖL FOLKÖL STARKÖL**

## How to Buy Beer in Sweden

Class I and II can be purchased in ordinary supermarkets. Class III, Mellanöl and Starköl, can only be bought either in Systembolaget or in bars and restaurants with a special license for alcohol sales.

## Order a *stor stark*, 'big strong'

If you feel really manly, you should go to a pub and order a "stor stark" which means a "big strong". This will underline your masculinity in a way that everyone around you easily understands it.

If you don't like beer, you can drink cider instead. More refreshing, more sweet, less manly. In gender-equal Sweden, you don't have to bother about those differentiations too much though, unless you're meeting your male friends to watch a football match maybe.

## How to order a beer in Sweden

*En öl, tack! - A beer, please!*
*En stor stark, tack! - A big strong, please!*

So, on your path to Swedishness, at least once, consider ordering a *stor stark* in a pub, or check the percentage of alcohol when a friend gives you a bottle or can at a party!

# 18. Be Able to Sing ABBA Songs

Have you ever heard of ABBA? Of course, you have! Stupid of me to even ask that question, right?

In case you didn't, ABBA is a music band from the 70's and 80's who have achieved outstanding international success. They even won the Eurovision Song Contest in 1974, with a song called "Waterloo". Even today, their songs are played all over the world on the radio and on parties where people like to dance good old disco style.

## Basic Knowledge About ABBA

Whenever you talk to a Swede about ABBA, you should know the following facts:

- ABBA are the initials for their band members: **A**gnetha Fältskog, **B**jörn Ulvaeus, **B**enny Andersson and **A**nni-Frid Lyngstad.
- The first two and the latter two were couples (not anymore though).
- ABBA has nothing to do with the Swedish producer of sea food, Abba, which has been longer 'on the market' than the band. Actually the band asked the food company if they could use the acronym 'ABBA' as their band name. The food company didn't mind and answered with a friendly letter and a can of tuna.
- ABBA declined a 1 billion-dollar offer for a reunion a couple of years ago.

## ABBA Spin-offs

Although they declined this immense amount of money, they still wrap their work in different ways, thereby they make a few extra Swedish Krona and keep their songs in people's memories. In the 90's, they promoted a cover band called A-Teens. There was also a movie called *Mamma Mia*, based on a musical with the same name.

You don't need to know the A-Teens songs or have been to the musical. But I strongly recommend you watch the movie. Every Swede has. That's why you should probably too.

## ABBA Museum

Since many Sweden-tourists have a big interest in ABBA and a wide open wallet, an ABBA museum has been built in Stockholm's old town, where you can see old ABBA dresses and other sparkling things.

They even installed a telephone that ABBA members ring once in a while and talk to random visitors. What would you ask or say, if you happen to be standing next to the phone when one of the As or Bs called?

## Sing Along an ABBA Song

ABBA songs have simple lyrics which makes them easy to remember. Ideal to sing along while driving or cooking. You might even experience this yourself when you're at a Swedish party, and the people around you start to sing along with an ABBA song, say, Gimme Gimme Gimme.

In other words, there's a lot of ABBA stuff going on in Sweden. As a new-Swede, you shouldn't feel embarrassed, just start to sing-along!

# 19. Swear Like a Swede

Normally, when Swedes make a mistake, they say words like *hopsan*, *oj* or *alltså näääh*.

But when they drop their iPhone or find out that their colleague has taken their mug from the office cabinet, stronger language can cross their lips.

Therefore, it's important, for you as a new-Swede, to understand the most common Swedish swear words and when to use them correctly.

## Most Popular Swedish Swear Words

People from your country probably use terms that are connected to genitals, or actions that are connected to the application of them. Swedes on the other hand, prefer to refer to the devil and the place where he's living.

## Top 3 Swedish Swear Words

1. *fan* - devil
2. *jävla* - devilish
3. *helvete* - hell

Another popular word is *skit* (shit), which you can freely combine with many other Swedish words, like *skitstövel* (shit-boot) or *skitbil* (shitty car) or *skitsamma* (never mind).

Once, when a friend caught his finger in a closing door, I witnessed rhetoric perfection as he managed to use all of the aforementioned words within just one sentenc: '*Fan i helvetes jävla skit!*' - 'Devil in hell's devilish shit!'

## Swedish Profanity

Of course, these are not the only Swedish swear words you can use to express your *irritation*. There are more words you should know - but you shouldn't use. Or, if you do, maybe only when your closest friends are around.

So, here are the super-rude words you shouldn't use when you meet your parents in law or a policeman or -woman. Yes, we're talking about those sexually related words standing for female and male genital organs.

Here we, go

- Female: The Swedish equivalent for, erm, '*cunt*' is: '*fitta*'
- The men's part, '*cock*' is simply '*kuk*' in Swedish. (Not to be confused with the Swedish word for chef: '*kock*')

## Nice Swedish Curse Word

Now that we have gone through very foul language - and I have stopped blushing - it's time to finish this *How to be Swedish*-step with a word you can use without being concerned, even when children are around. The nicest swear word in Sweden is: *sjutton* - seventeen. Yeah, I know, it sounds funny and maybe it's even a bit cute.

So, now you *jävla* soon to be Swede, know how to *fan* swear like a *hellvetes* Swede.

# 20. Know How to Prepare *Köttbullar*

Have you been to IKEA recently? If you had a delicious lunch there together with your partner or children, you probably considered ordering *köttbullar*.

When you ordered *köttbullar*, you might have pronounced the '*k*' of '*köttbullar'* with a '*k*'-sound. The correct version would be '*shöttbullar*' instead.

Most people don't know about that, most likely not even the waiter or waitress at the IKEA restaurant. But now that you know how to pronounce it correctly, don't correct him or her. Unless you want to risk getting that one meat ball he or she dropped on the floor a few minutes before.

## Popular Swedish Food

Swedes love their meatballs. This is why you, as a new-Swede, should know how to prepare their national dish. Even though, contrary to many Swedes' belief, this dish isn't even on the Top 10 list on the most popular in Sweden. The most popular dish in Sweden is Spaghetti with *köttfärssås* (mincemeat sauce).

Whenever you feel like having Swedish meatballs but don't want to go to IKEA and risk spending money on furniture and home decoration that you actually don't need, you should remember, you can easily prepare them yourself. No magic. Even I can do it. If you are a vegetarian or vegan or simply don't like to eat meat, just skip to the next chapter.

If you find yourself being a hungry carnivore, here is the recipe...

# Original Swedish Meatballs Recipe

Just follow the steps below and voila, your original Swedish meatballs can be served in no time.

## *Ingredients*

For 4–6 servings
- Some butter/oil for the pan
- 75 g (¾ cup) white breadcrumbs
- 500 g (18 oz) ground beef/pork mixture
- 250 ml (1¼ cup) milk
- 1 egg
- 1 onion
- Salt
- Pepper
- Ground allspice

## *Preparation, in 8 easy steps*

1. Soak the breadcrumbs in milk, for about 10 minutes.
2. In the meantime, dice the onion and fry gently in a little butter/olive oil without browning.
3. Blend the ground meat mixture with the onion, egg, milk/breadcrumb mixture and the spices.
4. Add salt and pepper. Continue blending for about 5-10 minutes. Add a little water if the mixture feels too firm. Check the taste by test-frying one meatball.
5. Then shape small meatballs with the aid of two spoons or with your hands – it's easier if you smear some butter in your hands to make the raw meatballs stick less. Place on clean plates.
6. Brown a pat of butter in a frying pan, and as soon as it 'goes quiet', place the meatballs in the pan and let them brown on all sides.
7. Shake the frying pan regularly.

8. Fry until meatballs have the desired color.

## What to serve with Swedish meatballs

Most Swedes serve *kokt potatis* (boiled potatoes) or potato
purée. But you can also combine it with French fries, egg
noodles or Spaghetti. Also, don't forget to add some raw stirred
lingonberries. This makes your plate look more colorful and
inviting.

Now that you have prepared and eaten your homemade
köttbullar, you can consider yourself a step closer to perfected
Swedishness - and apply for a position as chef at IKEA.

Disclaimer: No, IKEA didn't pay me anything to mention
them that often. Swedes mention IKEA even more often, and
most of them don't get paid either.

*Smaklig måltid! - Have a nice meal!*

# 21. Appreciate Flat Hierarchies

*"Hello Marie!"*
*"Hi, Peter! How are you doing today?"*
*"I'm good, thanks? How was your weekend, Marie?"*

What you've just read could have been an ordinary conversation between two Swedish friends or colleagues. But not only that. It also could have been a chat between a professor and one of her students. Or a cleaning staff member, emptying the garbage can in the office of the CEO.

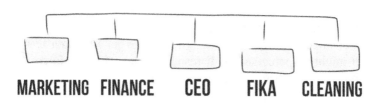

**MARKETING FINANCE CEO FIKA CLEANING**

## How to Address Swedes Correctly

A good indicator for flat Swedish hierarchies is the way Swedes address each other in conversations. Whenever you meet a person with authority in Sweden, you address him or her by their first name. No Mr. Norberg or Mrs. Lennartsson. No Professor Ericsson or Doctor Börjesson.

The only exception: members of the Swedish royal family still like to be called by their title. Say *kronprinzessan* (crown princess) instead of *Victoria*. Maybe good to know, if you happen to bump into her during a sightseeing tour in Stockholm's old town.

# Showing Respect

Don't misunderstand this social rule! Swedes may be less formal in their communication, but it doesn't mean they also are closer to each other. Just because you name people by their first name, it doesn't mean that you don't respect them and that you immediately can act like friends.

Swedes communicate closeness rather by the choice of topics they talk about and how much personal information they reveal to you.

On a Monday morning at the office, you might welcome your boss with "Hej Håkan", but you better not tell him about your terrible hangover you had yesterday.

What the culture of addressing everyone by their first name does is creating simplicity and a more welcoming atmosphere. It's easier to communicate.

To become more Swedish, you have to get over your fear that it might be perceived as disrespectful behavior to address your boss with Ann-Sofie. She is used to it.


# Showing Status Without Titles

Swedish people don't collect titles as eagerly as in other countries. Only a few Swedes can actually be perceived as show offs. (To observe some of them, you'd have to spend an evening at a square called *Stureplan*, in central Stockholm.)

In Swedish society, everyone has the same value (at least that's what they say they strive for). Of course not all are acting like it. But the idea is present and the majority of the Swedish people try to live up to it.

This "anti-show-off"-attitude is also based on two more cultural phenomenon or concepts, namely *jantelagen* and *lagom*. (I will get into these topics in a later chapter.)

## Flat Swedish Hierarchy

When employees have the feeling they have an influence on the company, that their opinion counts, then overall work-satisfaction is increased.

Bosses with an authoritarian attitude have no good standing in Swedish companies. It's very important to engage communication across employees and departments, and strive for *consensus*.

On the other hand, Swedish decision making can be slow, really slow. Trying to find consensus with almost every team member takes time.

So, dear soon to be Swede, if you talk to your boss in a Swedish company, or whenever a policeman stops you, it's ok to address them with 'Robert' or 'Josefin' – only, if those are their real names, of course. And don't forget to give some positive feedback!

# 22. Be Safety-Conscious

Good news for you, if you also prefer things to be safe: Sweden really is the right place for you!

Swedish safety-thinking can be found in many places products. For example, have a look at IKEA's assembly instructions - half of the pages are safety measures, showing you how to install that shelf in a way it won't tip over on your feet or cat. Yapp, those pages you usually skip reading.

## Not so Safe in Sweden

The two common areas Swedes are bad at when it comes to safety are: elevators and sex.

There are still a lot of elevators in Sweden without the inside door. Get your shoe laces stuck in the door and your shoes are likely to be torn off your feet. And don't hold the dog leash too loosely when you enter. You probably have already seen on YouTube what could happen to Ludde.

When it comes to sex, many Swedes take fewer precautions. No surprise then that the use of condoms isn't as widely spread as chlamydia.

Although only about 1% of the Swedish population is catholic, the majority of Swedes avoid condoms, even in casual encounters.

In 2007, the EU warned about a special type of chlamydia from Sweden, one that even got the name "Swedish chlamydia". This might explain why Sweden has been named *the sexually transmitted infection capital of Europe*.

## Essential Equipment for Being a *Safe Swede*

To compensate the risky behavior in bed, Swedes try to be a bit more safe on the street, by wearing a special safety-item, one you can find in almost every Swedish wardrobe: the popular *flexväst*, reflection vest.

To become a real Swede, you must own one and put it on whenever you walk outside in the dark.

Because of the rising popularity of the *flexväst*, almost all Swedish pedestrians, in winter, look like Minions.

## Safety at Work in Sweden

Safety is very important at workplaces as well. No one shall get home with a pain in the back or a nail in the forehead. Just have a look at a Swedish construction site. Everyone wears equipment that could protect them not only from minor injuries but potentially even from a minor nuclear fallout.

Next time you pass a Swedish construction site, have a look at the workers there. They usually work in groups of four people, each with a different task. While only one does the actual work, the other three have to take care of his safety.

*"Working in Sweden is likely to be more safe than staying in bed."*

So go ahead, dear soon to be Swede, be safe, go to work in Sweden - and put on a *flexväst*.

# 23. Buy a *Sommarstuga*

If you ever received a postcard from Sweden, it most likely depicted a beautiful landscape, with fields or forests, a lake and eventually, somewhere below a Swedish flag, a *röd stuga*, red cottage house.

## Swedish Summer House

Those red houses are not only placed on postcards, making you believe they are everywhere in Sweden - these houses really *are* everywhere. Well, of course not in the center of big cities. But you will certainly see one of those houses every few minutes when you drive along a country road. So don't rush taking a picture when you pass the first 'real Swedish house'.

## Own a *Sommarstuga*

There are nearly 600,000 summer houses in Sweden. And more than 50% of the population have access to at least one of them through family or friends.

You already have a house or an apartment in the city? A reasonable income? Then consider investing in a, *sommarstuga*, summer house.

*Sommarstugor* are very popular among Swedes who'd rather stay in their home country during summer. Many Swedes who live in the city, in a fancy apartment have a summer cottage they can easily get to within an hour. Those houses are usually situated at the coast or forest or in proximity to a lake. Often with a minimalist equipment, sometimes with a *utedass*, outhouse, a toilet outside the main house. The most expensive Swedish summer houses can be found on the islands of Stockholms *skärgård*, archipelagos.

## Why Swedes Have a *Summer-House Culture*

Many years ago, when there were no highways in Sweden and connections by plane or train didn't exist, Swedes had to find a way to go on vacation without spending half of their holiday time on the way to the destination. They took advantage of the cheap and widespread land and the plentiful construction material, wood, just outside the door, to build their sweet little red houses.

So, dear soon to be Swede, got some extra kronor put aside? Buy your own *sommarstuga*!

# 24. Be Bad at Small Talk

It's maybe not too uncommon that people get easily nervous when they have to talk to strangers. But what's different with the Swedes is that they even feel uncomfortable talking to people they have already met before.

## Talking to Strangers in Sweden

Swedes feel awkward when a stranger starts talking to them.

If you start talking to a foreign Swede on the street or when you sit next to him or her on a bus, you might be perceived as a weirdo. Swedes will reply politely and answer all your questions anyway. Just try to round up the conversation as soon as the Swede takes a longer look at the mobile phone while you're talking.

Swedes have many ways to avoid a small talk situation. Of course they can talk a little when they meet a friend. But when they meet someone that's just an acquaintance, they often do everything to avoid an awkward small talk conversation.

One trick to avoid talking to you is avoiding eye-contact. This can happen when a person you are familiar with passes by in the shopping street looking down on the phone or another direction. No worries, it's totally normal in Sweden. Don't take it personally, they do it with their fellow 'old-Swedes' as well.

Mastering 'Swedish eye-contact avoidance' gives you certain time efficiency advantages. Should you ever see a former one-night stand or boss walking in your direction, just stare at your phone or straight past him or her and pretend you haven't noticed that person. The other person definitely will do exactly the same to avoid *time-consuming small talk awkwardness.*

## Swedish Small Talk Topic

If you find yourself in a situation when your good manners tell you that you *have to* have a short conversation, choose the right topic to talk about.

You will make most Swedes feel uncomfortable talking about anything but weather, vacations, and maybe the food they carry in their shopping basket. "Oh you bought corn and minced meat - are you going to have a *tacco kväll* (taco evening)?"

After four or five sentences back and forth, a Swede will say, "då så" or "nähä" to indicate it's time to say goodbye. Or he or she will wish you to "ha det så bra!" (Lit. "have it so good!") and continue with the grocery shopping. Then, a minute later, you run into that same person again in front of the toilet paper shelf and, of course, try to avoid eye-contact. If your eyes happen to meet, just put on that well trained forced smile.

## Topics to Avoid

You'd best not talk about the following topics with those Swedes who you do not consider your closest friends, and definitely not in any small talk situation: politics, religion, disease or the delicious red wine you drank last Tuesday evening (because they might think you're an alcoholic if you drink during the week). Basically, just avoid any topic that could potentially create conflict or very unpleasant feelings.

So, dear soon to be Swede, whenever you meet old-Swedes, try to not talk about something that makes them feel awkward. Simply comment on the weather!

# 25. Fear *Magsjuka*

Everyone tries not to get ill. Including the Swedes. But there is one illness they particularly try to avoid, *magsjuka*, the stomach flu.

## What Happens When You Have *Magsjuka*?

This is when the content of your digestive system splits up in two parts. One leaves your body the way it entered while the other takes the backdoor. Both are in a hurry. This means *you* hurry to the bathroom regularly, and stay there for a while until you can return to your bed, drink tea and continue watching streamed movies from the internet.

## Stomach Flu in Sweden

It's not only an unpleasant clinical condition (for 1-3 days), it is also a bad thing to have, because people around you will treat and avoid you like a zombie.

In Sweden, you often hear the word *magsjuka* in connection with the following words...

- ... don't go to work!
- ... *äckligt* (disgusting)
- ... *handsprit* (hand sanitizer)
- ... where is the toilet?

Well, maybe not the last point, since people who have *magsjuka* and move around in public usually don't admit they have it.

# How to Create Space in Swedish Public Transport

Have some fun, go on public transport during rush hour. Pretend you're calling a friend and say loudly and clearly "My doctor just told me I have *magsjuka*". Then, enjoy the reactions of the people around you and pick your favorite seat.

So, dear soon to be Swede, be aware of *magsjuka*, use plenty of *handsprit* and hold your breath as long as someone stands closer than an arm's length in front of you, when you are in the *tunnelbana* (subway) or waiting in line at the grocery store!

# 26. Sing the Swedish Happy Birthday Song

Once a year Swedes celebrate their birthday. If you, as a new-Swede, ever consider celebrating your birthday, in the presence of other Swedes, there is something I need to warn you about...

Not only that it's YOU who has to prepare the food and plan the whole event (well, at least everyone will bring their own alcoholic drinks), but you also have to risk being exposed to the Swedish birthday song in full length with that extra '*hurra-thingy*' in the end.

## Swedish Birthday Tradition

At these kinds of occasions, Swedes tend to sing their birthday song (lyrics below). "That can't be too bad," you might think. But behold. The first minute of the song, you might even be surprised by the pleasant melody and the solid singing skills of your Swedish friends.

But then, towards the end, make yourself ready to experience an unexpected turn. Pop in your earplugs and hold your ears covered as soon as one of your guests starts shouting "*Ett fyrfaldigt han/hon leve ...*". This is the introduction to an eardrum erupting "*Hurra! Hurra! Hurra! Hurra!*".

Pretend not to be shocked, just smile and say "Tack!" (Thanks!). Then go to the bathroom and remove your earplugs.

## HURRA!

Depending on the time of the evening, and thereby the amount of alcohol consumed, the volume of this song and hurra-shouting may increase exponentially. It'll be the moment all your neighbors will know it's your birthday. And that you didn't invite them over. (Which is fine in Sweden, since your neighbors would rather watch *Melodifestivalen* on TV anyways.)

So, dear soon to be Swede, to know when to cover your ears, or what to sing at your friend's birthday, learn the Swedish happy birthday song…

Here are the lyrics:

*Ja, må han leva!*
*Ja, må han leva!*
*Ja, må han leva uti hundrade år!*
*Javisst ska han leva!*
*Javisst ska han leva!*
*Javisst ska han leva uti hundrade år!*
*Och när han har levat*
*Och när han har levat*
*Och när han har levat uti hundrade år!*
*Ja, då ska han skjutas*
*Ja, då ska han skjutas*
*Ja, då ska han skjutas på en skottkärra fram!*

Followed by...
*Ett fyrfaldigt han leve ...*
*HURRA! HURRA! HURRA! HURRA!*

(Above the version for a male birthday child. For the female version, replace *han* with *hon*.)

69

# 27. Give a Red Dala Horse to Sweden Visitors

This can be found in every Swedish souvenir-shop. One of the most iconic national symbols of Sweden: the *dalahäst*, Dala horse. It is mostly colored in red, decorated with *kurbits* pattern, twisting plants and flowers. (I have one on my desk, right next to my Swedish flag and mini-midsummer pole.)

Those sweet little horses usually find their new homes in the shelves of people who either have been to Sweden themselves or know someone who has.

*"As a real Swede, you should consider the Dala horse as one of the most typical Swedish things anyone who has some kind of connection to Sweden can have at home in their Billy shelf."*

## Origin of the Dala Horse

Sweden is full of trees. Many years ago, wood-workers from the Swedish province of Dalarna were having a break from wood working, sitting on a tree trunk, being bored. They decided to do something entertaining, (back then they didn't have a mobile phone and thereby no access to Facebook, Instagram or Aftonbladet.se) so they looked around for some inspiration on what they could do. What they saw was nothing but wood and horses. Suddenly, one wood worker said, *'let's make wooden horses'*. So they did, and took them home to the children.

Later, when the children grew up and had no use for the horses anymore, they took them to *Gamla Stan* (old town) in Stockholm and sold them to Sweden tourists. Probably.

The world's largest *dalahäst* is 13 meters/43 feet high and can be seen at the junction of Swedish national roads 70/68 in Avesta.

## Dala Horse as a Present

If you, as a new-Swede, ever receive a present from an old-Swede, chances are high that you might get a Dala horse. If your Swedish friends know that you already have one, you'll probably just get flowers or a bottle of wine instead.

So, dear soon to be Swede, consider giving away a Dala horse to someone who has at some point expressed that he or she likes Sweden!

# 28. Be Proud of Your Viking Ancestry

The Americans have Cowboys, the Japanese have Samurais, the Brits have Mister Bean, and the Swedes - well, they have the Vikings.

Vikings are the personified symbols of the Swedish nation. You find them in diverse ways in Swedish souvenir shops, in movies and or as names of sports teams. Other Scandinavian countries also use them for diverse marketing purposes, but, since the title of this book is *How to be Swedish* and not *How to be Scandinavian*, let's just choose to think of them as mainly Swedish for the moment.

## Basic Viking Knowledge

Vikings were in their prime during the late 8th to late 11th centuries, when they raided and traded from Scandinavia across wide areas of northern, central and eastern Europe. The Vikings were also good at building boats with a flat keel. This made it easier for them to travel way up rivers, access shores, and thus spend more time sunbathing on beaches and plundering villages.

*Vikingarna* (Vikings) were wild and rough and had long beards. Many modern Swedes still have long beards.

Vikings believed in several gods and drank a lot of alcohol. Nowadays, Swedes have given up believing in too many gods, if any. But they are still going strong keeping up their good old drinking traditions.

Yes, the Vikings took the ladies from the conquered villages and made them their wives. Rumor has it, they only took the good looking blonde women with them. According to a few drunk Swedes, this is the explanation why there are so many blondes in Sweden. Well, at least it sounds somewhat plausible and like a good story to share when you're drunk.

## Did Vikings wear horns on their helmets?

No, they didn't. I was disappointed, too, when I found out. This memorable item finds its origin in a theater performance from the early 1900's. Actors, dressed as Vikings, were given a helmet with horns. From then on, every Viking has been depicted with a horny helmet.

So, dear soon to be Swede, be proud of 'your' Viking ancestors and start spreading these rumors!

# 29. Dream of Living Abroad, for a While

Sweden is a small country. Not that small actually, at least when it comes to land area (450,295 km2 /175,896 sq mi). But with a population of about 10 million, Sweden is considerably small.

Although the country of Sweden is unarguably beautiful, Swedes tend to dream about living somewhere else. At least for a period of time.

## Why Swedes Want to Go Somewhere Else

Well, first of all, Sweden is a bit cold and dark in winter which is why Swedes prefer to go to more southern and sunny places. Then, Swedes consider themselves as *lite tråkiga*, a bit boring, therefore they seek a surrounding with more "passionate" and "energetic" people in countries with a more expressive culture. Often, Swedes simply want to feel free and discover the world, much like their Viking ancestors.

## Where to Go

You as a new-Swede, should get used to conversations with old-Swedes in which they tell you that they would love to work in a sunny country during the winter, and then come back to live in Sweden during summer.

Many Swedes have made traveling experiences right after school or after finishing their studies. Particularly those in their late teens or twenties will tell you that they want to travel through Australia in a mini-bus, work as an au pair or do an internship in the United States - especially in Los Angeles or New York – and then go backpacking in South America or work as a bartender in London.

So, dear soon to be Swede, pick a destination for your desired three month (or longer) trip: Australia, London, New York, Los Angeles or South America. And if you prefer beaches, add Thailand to your list as an alternative.

Once you have reached your travel destination, don't forget to update your Facebook cover image or profile picture, showing you walking over Brooklyn Bridge, standing on top of Machu Picchu or lying on the roof of a Volkswagen minibus somewhere in the Australian desert.

# 30. Get a Swedish Personal Identity Number

In pretty much all countries in the world, people have names. Using names is a great way to make it easier for people to understand whether you are talking to or about them in conversations. Names also make it easier to identify someone when looking for additional information in a data base.

Swedes don't have a large pool of first or last names to choose from, for example many are called Johan Andersson or Anna Johnsson. Since many Swedes have identical names, they can easily get confused with each other. This is probably one of the reasons why Sweden introduced the *personnummer*-system.

## Swedish *Personnummer*, Personal Identity Number

Every Swede gets a personal identity number. Those numbers are issued by *Skatteverket*, the Swedish Tax Agency, as part of the population register.

A personal number can look like this: 890627-3254. Ten digits which represent your birthday and four extra digits. In the example above: year '89, month June (06), day 27th, and the last four digits.

The last four digits are determined partly by the place of your registration (usually where you're born in Sweden), your gender and the very last digit is the result of some kind of weird algorithm.

## Use Your Personnummer

As soon as you, dear soon to be Swede, have received a *personnummer*, it's time to learn it by heart. Actually you don't have to put too much effort into learning your number at home since you will have to repeat it so many times in your life in Sweden, that it's difficult not to remember it.

Since even companies can request personal information from *Skatteverket* about you, like for example your address, you might simply be asked for your personal identity number when you order something on the internet, sign a mobile phone contract or book an appointment with your doctor.

So, dear soon to be Swede, if you haven't yet, it's time to apply for your *personnummer*! The person with the coolest four extra digits wins.

# 31. Get Used to Swedish Healthcare

Are you considering moving to Sweden? If you want to go to Sweden, become Swedish and consider getting ill once in a while - due to a virus or an annoying boss - I have good and bad news for you...

The good news: Swedish health care is not expensive. Bad news: You get what you pay for.

## Basic Health Care at (Almost) No Extra Costs

Basic healthcare is included in the Swedish welfare system for everyone who is a resident in Sweden. This means that even if you are an expat living in Sweden for at least 12 months, you are covered. (Don't forget to register at *Försäkringskassan* first.)

Health and even dental care is subsidized by the Swedish tax payers. Cost ceilings are put in place for healthcare services: A limit on individual contributions to health care of 1100 Swedish crowns per year. Once this limit is reached, all other healthcare services are free of charge for a 12-month period since the first payment (called *högkostnadskydd*). Even for prescribed medication, you have to pay no more than 2200 crowns per year.

# Standard Procedures and Waiting Times

The flu is very common in Sweden in Autumn and Spring. Many people catch it and so will you. To make the flu go over bit faster, some Swedes believe it might be a good idea to consult a doctor. And it certainly is, considering you only pay a 100-300 SEK fee for a visit.

Then you have about 10-30 minutes waiting time, which you can share with other coughing flu patients in the waiting room, while staring at a heart-attack-detection poster or a bored gold fish in an aquarium.

After that, not the doctor does welcome you. No, the Swedish health care system is so efficient, a nurse with a soft voice and well trained polite smile will welcome you and guide you to the examination room for the first part of the audition process. The nurse checks if you're ill enough to talk to the doctor later that day or, more likely, tomorrow.

# "Let's Try Alvedon® First"

About 95% of the times you talk to a nurse, at the end of the conversation you will hear: *Avvakta lite och ta en Alvedon*, (Wait a little while and take an Alvedon). This is probably the all-time most said sentence in every Swedish *vårdcentral* (healthcare center).

Alvedon: the super medication against almost everything. Every treatment of even the worst disease probably at some point started with a Swedish nurse recommending the intake of Alvedon, which is basically just a pain killer.

# Waiting Time and Job Opportunities

Urgent cases or emergencies are always prioritized and treated immediately, of course.

Although the national guarantee of care, *vårdgaranti*, states that you should have to wait no more than 7 days for a visit to a primary care physician, and no more than 90 days for a visit to a specialist, it regularly happens that the Swedish healthcare system can't deliver within that period. But hey, it's almost for free.

Specialists are demanded in Sweden. If you are a doctor, you might easily find your future career in this Nordic country. Nurses and people for elderly care are also highly demanded. Great job opportunities for you then, if you have no problems getting exposed to or even in touch with blood or poo on a daily base.

So, dear soon to be Swede, be patient with/of the Swedish health care system!

# 32. Be Nice to the Environment

Swedes love to get out in nature, hiking, skiing, swimming or sunbathing on the grass. To make these outdoor experiences as pleasant as possible, Swedes commonly understand that it's better to preserve the beautiful Swedish nature and fight everything that could possibly have a negative impact on it.

## Buy Things that are Good for the Nature

Before Swedes makes a purchase, they carefully check packages for labels that indicate that the product has been produced under environmentally friendly conditions.

> *"Swedes have a built in must-buy reflex when being presented to products that are labelled "bra för miljön" (good for the environment), or contains the word "miljävänligt" (environmentally friendly)".*

These labels successfully give Swedes the good conscience that they have actively contributed to make the world a better place. Those environment labels are almost as appealing to Swedes as a sign that says *REA* (sales).

## Recycle in the *Miljöhus*

To throw away your garbage, you have to go to a little shed outside your apartment building. It's called the *miljöhus*, literally 'environment house'. In there you find open containers for different types of garbage: clear glass, colored glass, plastic, card board, metal, food waste, batteries, light bulbs, radioactive waste and one universal container for everything else.

These containers are open, so you can easily find the *miljöhus* by following the smell of rotten garbage.

To correctly recycle, some Swedes consider it important to clean their plastic yoghurt mug before they throw it away. That's probably the most committed way anyone can contribute to environmental preservation, isn't it?

2 glasses of clear water.
1 bucket of nutritious soil.
And for desert, 1 gallon of pollution free air.
I think our Swedish chef can fix that.

So, dear soon to be Swede, it's time to practice your ability to fold boxes and cartons so they take up a minimum amount of space, and throw them into the right container in your *miljöhus*!

# 33. Make Use of the *Allemansrätten*

Something typically Swedish, if you ask a Swede, is not only köttbullar, lagom and Ikea, but also a special right called *allemansrätten* - the right of public access.

The right of public access is written in the constitution of Sweden: *Alla ska ha tillgång till naturen, (Everyone shall have access to nature)*.

This right gives you permission to go wherever you want and camp wherever you want, for one night. Any field, forest or your neighbor's garden. Well, actually you can not camp in your neighbor's garden unless he gives you permission to do so, but you are allowed to cross his or her fields and forest without asking. If you decide to stay in a nice spot in Swedish nature, you might want to contact the owner and just check if it's *okej* for them.

Then, once you have permission, just put up your tent and follow the rule "*don't disturb and don't destroy*".

You are even allowed to pluck berries or mushrooms, not to earn some extra money at the next food market though, but for personal consumption.

So, dear soon to be Swede, get your baskets out and start picking blueberries and *kantareller* (chanterelles)!

# 34. Avoid Opening a Can of *Surströmming*

## Don't Read this While Eating!

In some countries, horses are considered a delicacy. In some regions of the world, people like to prepare a good salad refined with insects. In Sweden, you might get served not only moose meat, but also a fermented herring, *surströmming*.

Surströmming has a very intense odor. It stinks a lot. Some say, it actually tastes ok, but you shouldn't inhale while taking it into your mouth. Try it out. If you don't like it, just have a *snaps* right after.

## How Surströmming Smells

It is possible to replicate the smell of Surströmming almost accurately: Take an old pair of running shoes, fill them with onions, garlic, asparagus, raw meat, dog poo and a slice of cheese. Then put it into a black plastic bag and seal it. Store it in direct sunlight so the bag can heat up to about 100°C/212°F.

After about one week, open the plastic bag and enjoy!

## Advice for Dog Owners

There are plenty of videos on the internet, where people challenge themselves smelling and eating pieces of *surströmming*. Despite my own expectations, dogs with their hyper-sensitive noses, surprisingly, seem to like the smell of *surströmming*, a lot. I prove it in a YouTube clip: 'Dogs try *Surströmming*', (just search for that title). One dog got so excited, he fell from the table.

If you have a dog that tends to be lazy and boring – open a can of rotten Swedish fish – and see what happens.

## Swedish Friends

Immediately break up any friendship with a person who tells you, it's ok to open a can of *surströmming* indoors. Once you've opened a can of this rotten fish, you'll understand why. Usually, nice people tell you to eat it outside only. Some airlines even forbid you to carry it on a plane. In case a can explodes the juice of this stinky fish spreads all over the luggage, or, even worse, imagine if this happens in the passenger area.

So, dear soon to be Swede, try *surströmming* at least once, and then tell all newly arriving Sweden tourists that they have to try it as well some time! ... Indoors. ;)

# 35. Drink Plenty of Strong Coffee

Winters in Sweden are long and dark. (It feels like I'm repeating myself now.) Long winter darkness may lead to tiredness, low energy and a lack of passion. To get some extra energy and heat, Swedes found *kaffe*, coffee, to be their drink of choice.

## Strong Swedish Coffee

Swedes really love their coffee. Drinking coffee is an essential part of their daily routine. One in the morning, several at work, a Cappuccino during meetings with friends and in the evening, an Espresso to avoid falling asleep during an episode of *Wallander*.

You find coffee places and cafés everywhere in Sweden. But beware, Swedes don't drink their coffee the way you use to in your old country.

Swedish coffee is strong. Very strong. So strong indeed that when you pour your standard amount of milk into it, you will realize your coffee will hardly change its color. Basically, you can consider normal Swedish coffee a bit stronger than Espresso and a little weaker than tar.

## Coffee Facts

Increase your coffee intake gradually until you hit the Swedish average of 3,2 cups a day.

Once you're used to it, every other coffee in the world will taste like black colored water.

*"Three of four Swedes drink coffee every day."*

The average 3,2 cups of coffee every day puts Swedes in the second place of the highest coffee consumption in the world, right after 3,5 cups that the Finns drink daily. The other Scandinavian countries, Norway and Denmark, also belong to the biggest coffee consumers, both with 3,1 cups per day.

So, dear soon to be Swede, get your digestive system prepared for your 3,2 cups of strong Swedish coffee per day!

# 36. Play an Outdoor Game Called *Kubb*

For many Swedes, being outside in the sun, sitting in a *brassestol*, a little deckchair, having a beer or cider while having a BBQ is a desirable experience. But it can become a bit boring at times.

The problem with most lawn activities is, you have to put your beer bottle or can down to compete. Swedes don't want to do that. So they came up with a game called *Kubb*. A game that allows them to join a competition while engaging in conversations and holding their drink in one hand, all at the same time.

## What's Kubb All About?

*Kubb* is a rather static game. Essentially, you have two teams, with each team having wooden, square-shaped blocks lined up in front of them. Then you have further round batons that one team throws at the blocks of the other team. (I probably already lost your attention there.) When all of the opponent's blocks are knocked down, the last step to victory is to hit the King, standing in the middle of the field.

Beware: there's always some Swedish person that argues about how many throwing attempts the leading team has to hit the king.

*"Kubb is like a blend of volleyball, chess and bowling. But with a little less sweat, brain and grace."*

Kubb can be played by old and young, sober and drunk. Little skill and lots of luck determines whether a baton hits a block after twisting through the air or bouncing on the grass, which is usually accompanied by the participants' *"Ooohhh!"* or *"Aaahhhh!"*.

Sounds like a weird game? Well, it takes some time to really appreciate its slowness.

Advantage: the rules are simple. You'll learn it quickly. After 10 minutes, you'll be almost as good as those who have played it for years. So everyone can join. A very Swedish game then.

So, on your way to Swedishness, enjoy playing *Kubb*, your soon to be favorite outdoor/drinking activity, with low risk of spillage!

# 37. Enjoy Paying Tax

Of course Swedes don't love to give away money, nevertheless they can appear a bit greedy when it comes to food and alcohol invitations. But then, food and alcohol is expensive in Sweden. So, don't expect to be invited for a restaurant visit or a cocktail by your Swedish friends too often. (Unless you have invited them first.)

## Tax on Alcohol

Alcohol is expensive because the state wants to have a big lump of the 100 SEK (about 10 EUR) that you pay for a bottle of red wine. About 60% go to the state's pockets.

## Swedish Income Tax

If you are among the lucky or hardworking ones with a high income above 5,000 Euros per month, you can expect to pay over 50% income tax. This is because the Swedish state cannot finance its expenses only on the population's alcohol consumption.

## Benefits of High Tax in Sweden

In Sweden, most benefits are financed by the *folkhemmet*, "people's' home", the governmental institutions. These include services which you normally pay for privately in your old country. Like for example, healthcare or education.

So, dear soon to be Swede, enjoy the benefits of the *folkhemmet* and enjoy financing it by paying a high tax!

# 38. Stop Bothering About Secrecy and Privacy

Do you like to share your age with unknown people? Would you mind if anyone checked the results from your previous studies just by calling your university? Did you answer these questions with yes? Well, then it's time to adjust to the Swedish view on privacy.

## Who is Driving that Car in Front of Me?

Anyone in Sweden can check the name and resident city of the owner of a vehicle just by sending an SMS with the registration number to the traffic agency. The system replies with the requested information. Great if someone parked on your personal parking lot, or if you want to get in touch with that person who you had this intense eye-contact with when you stopped at the traffic lights.

## Consider it Ok that Your Personal Information isn't Private at All

The Swedish government and all state organisations follow a principle called the *offentlighetsprincipen*, (openness principle). Regulated by the *tryckfrihetsförordning*, (freedom of press regulation), it says that all public records have to be documented and made accessible to anyone.

For example, any Swede can call your old university and ask for the results on your exams, without having to state one's name. The employer of the organisation isn't even allowed to ask for what reason you request this information.

Generally, this principle was found to give the public the opportunity to control state processes.

Of course, there are processes that only few people have access to, like state defence operations. So don't expect to be able to replace your bedtime thrillers with public state documents.

If someone knows your first name, last name and city of residence, they can easily find out the following information about you as well: full name, full address, phone number, relationship status and date of birth.

So, dear soon to be Swede, get used to giving an honest answer whenever anyone asks you for your age!

# 39. Be Proud of Swedish Innovations

Because of the forces of nature, darkness and cold, Swedes spend a substantial time of the year indoors sitting on minimalistic wooden chairs. While doing that, some Swedes think about how they can improve the world.

A couple of times this procedure has led to rather extraordinary innovations.

Below is a list of innovations you have or haven't heard about before. However, it's good advice to learn them by heart, so you can impress your Swedish friends next time you talk about your favorite conversation topics, like ball gearing or milk cartons:

## Innovations and Their Innovators from Sweden

- Dynamite - Alfred Nobel
- Boat propeller - Jonas Wenström
- Refrigerator - Carl Munter and Baltazar von Platen

"Swedes also invented the zip-fastener, to accelerate the process of getting each other out of their clothes"

- Zip fastener - Gideon Sundbäck
- Celsius - a scale for measuring temperature, by Anders Celsius
- Ball bearing - Sven Wingquist
- Milk carton - Ruben Rausing

# Further Innovations, or Rather Popular Products from Sweden

- Unassembled furniture in a flat pack - some guy at Ikea
- Skype - Niklas Zennström (and Janus Friis, from Denmark)
- Spotify - Daniel Ek and Martin Lorentzon

## Made in Sweden

Some products and even people that are "Made in Sweden" are internationally popular. As a new-Swede, you should pay attention and give credit to their success. Whenever you watch TV or a Hollywood movie, it is your task to first spot and then comment on the appearance of any *Saab* or *Skarsgård*.

So, dear soon to be Swede, don't forget to mention that certain innovations are from Sweden whenever a related topic comes up in conversations with foreigners!

# 40. Get a Swedish First- & Last Name

Every Swede has at least two names. A first- and a last name.

Swedes haven't been very innovative in the process of creating names, though. More than one third of all Swedish surnames end with *–son*. Those names are so common, that you will probably find at least one of them on the mailboxes of each Swedish apartment building.

## List of 10 Most Common Swedish Surnames

Minor name variations, for example *Karlsson* and *Carlsson,* are summarized under the variation that is most common, here Karlsson. (2015)

| Rank | Surname | Amount |
|------|---------|--------|
| 1 | Andersson | 241 854 |
| 2 | Johansson | 241 685 |
| 3 | Karlsson | 214 920 |
| 4 | Nilsson | 165 106 |
| 5 | Eriksson | 143 219 |
| 6 | Larsson | 120 795 |
| 7 | Olsson | 109 964 |
| 8 | Persson | 104 111 |
| 9 | Svensson | 97 761 |
| 10 | Gustafsson | 94 403 |

# What Typical Swedish Last Names Mean

The following words appear often in Swedish names and refer mostly to nature.

Ström – stream (river)
Berg – mountain/hill
Lind – linden
Ek – oak
Sjö – lake/sea
Sund – sea gate/strait
Å – small stream/creek
Ö – island
Björk – birch
Ny – new
Söder – south
Lund – small forrest
Gren – branch
Fors – cataract
Vik – bay
Holm – little island
Qvist/Kvist – twig

# Top 10 Swedish First-Names for Girls and Boys

If you don't like your current first-name, you might fancy one of the top 10 Swedish girl and boy names from following list. Names given to newborns in 2015:

| Rank | Female first name | Amount | Male first names | Amount |
|------|-------------------|--------|------------------|--------|
| 1 | Elsa | 872 | William | 977 |
| 2 | Alice | 847 | Lucas | 802 |
| 3 | Maja | 674 | Liam | 752 |
| 4 | Saga | 671 | Oscar | 737 |
| 5 | Ella | 627 | Elias | 732 |
| 6 | Lilly | 613 | Hugo | 711 |
| 7 | Olivia | 583 | Oliver | 709 |
| 8 | Ebba | 576 | Charlie | 664 |
| 9 | Wilma | 575 | Axel | 627 |
| 10 | Julia | 574 | Vincent | 602 |

So, dear soon to be Swede, if you want to get a more Swedish sounding name, feel inspired by the list above!

# 41. Have a *Fredagsmys*

Swedes take their work very seriously. They come on time. They leave on time. To get some recovery from a stressful workweek, some Swedish people decided to introduce a relaxing activity on Fridays, called *fredagsmys*, literally 'Friday cosiness'.

## How to *Fredagsmys*

Ideally, a *fredagsmys* happens right after having tacos for dinner. Having tacos for dinner is called a *taccokväll*, taco evening. This is a great compromise if two people in a relationship can't agree on what to eat that evening.

Finding the right food for a (hopefully) romantic and relaxing Friday tends to be less difficult than finding a TV show or movie both parts agree on.

## Fredagsmys Snacks

Important: Don't forget some crunchy snacks! Crisps are widely associated with a *Fredagsmys* in Sweden. Rumor has it that a crisps producer (OLW®) came up with the idea of *fredagsmys* to promote their snacks. Their TV advertisement was underlined with a catchy melody that every Swede knows *'Nu är det freeedagsmyyys... '*. Just ask a Swede and they will hum it for you (with slight embarrassment).

So, dear new-Swede, it's Friday (soon), put on your comfy sweatpants and gather with other family members or your partner in front of your TV and satisfy your need for snacks, entertainment and cuddling!

# 42. Find it Difficult to Receive a Favor

Most Swedes have good personal qualities. For example, they can be generous and welcoming. Plus, many Swedish people have a good memory.

In combination, this means that Swedes remember that you invited them for a beer a long time ago, and that they haven't had the opportunity to invite you back since then. This circumstance - the feeling of being in debt to someone – may give your Swedish friend a feeling of discomfort or, at worst, anxiety.

## Invitation from a Swede

When you're out for drink with a Swede, it's completely fine if you invite them for a beer. But have a look at their face when you give the invitation - saying you pay the bill - your Swedish friend will have the same expression as a student trying to memorize vocabulary.

If he won't have the chance to invite you to something that same evening, he will take care to equalize his debt next time you meet, even if that is just for a fika. You invited him for a beer in a Swedish pub before? Expect the best latte macchiato with cream and syrup in return. Remember, alcohol is expensive in Sweden.

Even if you're driving along in your friend's car, you should offer to pay back half of the gasoline costs. This might sound weird in many countries but in Sweden this is completely normal. Even my close Swedish friends regularly ask me how much they owe me after driving them to the city, a distance less than 5km/3.1mi.

## Without Debt

For Swedes, it's important not to bother anyone. To not take without giving back.

At first, this might look like grasping, greediness, but basically, it's just so they don't end up in indebted relationships with others.

One very Swedish way to reduce the feeling of guilt in situations of receiving a favor, is to say *thank you*, a lot: "*Tack, tack, tack-tack!*"

So, dear soon to be Swede, if an old-Swede ever invites you for something, don't forget to return the favor within an appropriate time... say, the same evening or at the latest, next time you meet for a fika.

In very urgent cases, for example, when you already know you're not going to see your friend for a while, consider saying to your friendly friend that you can "*swisha tillbaks pengarna*", meaning "paying back with the money transfer app Swish". Your friend will politely reply, "*No, I invited you!*" yet he will remember that you should pay next time you're out together.

# 43. Pick a Typical Swedish Sport

Swedish people are rather active in their leisure time. They like to *motionera*, 'move' or 'be active'.

In case you consider 'having a walk' a bit boring and prefer to compete, you can choose from an array of sports to 'be active' like a typical Swede.

## Popular Swedish Sports

Highly popular sports in Sweden that are regularly covered by the media:

### Football

Many Swedes, mostly men, like to talk about football. Whenever you hear a Swede talking about football with a person from another country, you can count the seconds until he leads the conversation to Zlatan. (If a football-Swede talks to a German, they never forget to mention the 4:4 draw of the game Sweden against Germany in Berlin, 2012.)

Among Swedish football fans, Zlatan has reached superstar status. I guess I'm not going too far if I say that the it has an equally high social status among Swedes as much as ABBA, Ingvar Kamprad (the founder of IKEA) or even Pippi Longstocking.

Another great event of Swedish football history: third place in the World Cup 1994, in the United States. Players of that team still appear regularly as commentators on TV, often trying hard to avoid comparing the current game too much with their own successes back in the glory days.

## Ice Hockey

It's not that surprising that ice hockey has become so popular when there are thousands of lakes spread all over the country, and winters are long and icy. Nowadays, you find an ice hockey center in almost every bigger city in Sweden.

Sweden's biggest hockey idol: '*Foppa*', Peter Forsberg.

The Swedish Ice hockey team, *Tre Kronor* (three crowns) has won Olympic gold in 1994 and several World Championships.

# More Sports

Alternatives if you don't like to run after a ball or hold a club in your hand:

For those Swedes who like to jump, run fast or throw things far away, there's *athletics*. The flexible Swedes do *gymnastics*. Those Swedes who like to get wet, *swim*. And others who like to take care of an animal while being active find their luck on the back of *horses*.

# (Weird) Swedish Sports

Popular Swedish Sports that you haven't heard of before:

## Innebandy

If you have thought about playing hockey, but tend to stumble while skating or don't like the idea of constantly wearing bulky, smelly equipment and a helmet that ruins your stylish haircut, *innebandy* might be just right for you. No special equipment needed, just a club that looks like a lightweight ice hockey club and a plastic ball. And off you go.

> *"Sweden is regularly world champions in Innebandy. But then, it's not really difficult to be world champion in a game no other nation has a clue about."*

## Orientering

*Orientering* (orienteering) actually really is cross-country running. It's about running a course, outside in the nature, often through a forest, looking for check-points marked on a map, as fast as possible. At each check-point, one must collect a stamp to prove that one has run the whole course. No mobile phone with Google maps allowed. You're only equipped with an old fashioned map and a compass.

It is a sport Swedes like to do with the whole family. If one family member gets lost in the vast Swedish forests, they still have a compass to find their way back to parking lots where the family is already collectively waiting, silently sitting in their Volvo.

So, dear soon to be Swede, get rid of some extra calories and start collect bruisers!

# 44. Hoist the Swedish Flag

Sweden offers a high quality of life: reasonably high wages, relatively low unemployment, a low rate of crime, high gender equality and high level of sustainability. No need to mention free schools and universities, good healthcare and at least 25 days off from work each year.

Even the technical infrastructure is highly advanced, for example with fast internet. Also, many Swedes have the latest mobile phones and computers - and they actually know how to use them.

All this makes Swedes very proud of their country. They might not show it directly to visitors or new-Swedes, but behind closed doors, some Swedes like to express their conviction that they live in the best country in the world.

## The Swedish Flag

To celebrate their beloved country, Swedes like to hoist their flag. But they not only hoist their flag on flagpoles, they put them everywhere: on napkins, birthday cards, graduation cards, toothpicks etc.

## Blå Gul

Isn't it nice, the Swedish flag? Ok, it's not really fancy. Just a yellow cross on blue ground.

Originally, the Swedish flag was based on the very first flag that represented a country, the Danish flag. The colors, blue and yellow, stem from the Wasa dynasty, in the 16th century.

# Flag Days in Sweden

On these days, you can expect to see the Swedish flag on all poles countrywide.

| Date | Swedish Name | English Name |
|---|---|---|
| 1 January | Nyårsdagen | New Year's Day |
| 28 January | Konungens namnsdag | Name day of the King |
| 12 March | Kronprinsessans namnsdag | Name day of the Crown Princess |
| First Sunday after the first full moon on or after 21 March | Påskdagen | Easter Sunday |
| 30 April | Konungens födelsedag | Birthday of the King |
| 1 May | Första maj | May Day |
| Seventh Sunday after Easter Sunday | Pingstdagen | Pentecost |
| 6 June | Sveriges Nationaldag | National Day of Sweden |
| Saturday between 20 June and 26 June | Midsommardagen | Midsummer Day |
| 14 July | Kronprinsessans födelsedag | Birthday of the Heir Apparent |

| 8 August | Drottningens namnsdag | Name day of the Queen |
|---|---|---|
| Second Sunday of September (every fourth year) | Dag för val till riksdagen | Election Day |
| 24 October | FN-dagen | United Nations Day |
| 6 November | Gustav Adolfsdagen | Gustavus Adolphus Day |
| 10 December | Nobeldagen | Alfred Nobel Day |
| 23 December | Drottningens födelsedag | Birthday of the Queen |
| 25 December | Juldagen | Christmas Day |

So, dear soon to be Swede, hoist the Swedish flag, and enjoy its color-matching with the heaven and the sun!

# 45. Drink (Alcohol) Like a Swede

*"Swedes are like bottles of vodka: From the outside they seem unexcited, calm, pure like water, colorless. But once they open up, you'll likely detect a slight smell of alcohol."*

In order to get hydrated, everyone has to drink water. In the eyes or rather the mouths of some people, water tastes a bit boring. Which is why they might prefer to get their body hydration through milk, soda or juice. Swedes, on the other hand, find milk, soda and juice a bit boring, because those drinks don't take them any closer to a state of tipsiness or even drunkenness. And drunkenness is what Swedes aim for - well, at least on the weekends.

## Systembolaget

Many, many years ago, workers in the mines and forest were partly paid in *brännvin*, spirits. Alcoholism became an increasing problem. Thus, the sales of alcohol were strongly regulated by the government. Until today, the sale of alcoholic drinks containing more than 3,5% is only allowed in *Systembolaget*, the state-owned alcohol monopoly. Of course you can buy Vodka and other alcoholic beverages in restaurants, pubs and night clubs, but for home consumption, you have to go to *Systemet*, as the Swedes colloquially call it.

## Expensive alcohol

Examples for expensive alcohol in Swedeh: a bottle of Absolut Vodka, 0,7 l, costs about 25 Euro. That's half the price of what you pay in Germany. Reason enough for many Swedes to drive through Denmark and take the ferry to a German Bordershop.

# Swedish Drinking Culture

*"All Swedes are alcoholics?! Certainly not! Only 4,4% of them are."*

Swedes have an ambivalent relationship towards alcohol. On one hand, they condemn it and its potential destructive effects on health and families. On the other hand, many Swedes enjoy getting drunk a few times per month.

It's common to see drunk people on late evenings in the city centers. Swedes don't look down at these people. Being drunk at certain times is accepted through all social classes in Sweden.

# When to Drink

It's not ok to drink during the week, before workdays, say Monday to Thursday and Sundays. Maybe a beer or a wine in the evening is *okej*, but you should certainly not do that every day unless you don't mind your colleagues suspecting you to be a *smyg alcoholist*, silent alcoholic.

Then on a Friday or Saturday evening it's totally fine to drink and get drunk. As much as you want.

Generally, it's accepted to drink when you go out and meet friends on a pre party. You might even get critical comments if you chose to party without having a drink. *Vad?! Ska du inte dricka ikväll?* (What?! You're not going to drink tonight?!) Is something you're likely to hear from a friend who sees you drinking out of a small plastic soda bottle that does NOT smell like you blended it with alcohol.

*Words from a Swede: "Of course one can have fun without being drunk. But it's stupid to miss the chance."*

## Two Sides of a Swede - Sober and Drunk

The Swedes you meet on a daily basis often show a completely different side of themselves when being drunk. Not necessarily in a bad way. The normally so shy and distant seeming Swedes suddenly dare to raise their voices, express conflicting opinions and start using extroverted body language while under the influence of alcohol.

The state of being drunk is not considered an unpleasant side effect, but rather a goal. A state that releases them from restrictions and allows them to show their real (drunk) self. It is acceptable to shout out your favorite song at night, to hit on that attractive person from your old work place that you coincidentally meet at a bar or send a *fylle sms*, 'drunk sms', to your ex saying you miss those great moments you had together. All this is, of course, is not possible when being sober.

However, once they're sober after a night of heavy drinking, Swedes feel *fylleångest*, anxiety from having done embarrassing things last night.

*"If you ever do something embarrassing in Sweden, no problem, your Swedish friends won't blame you too much - as long as you can blame it on the alcohol."*

# Don't Take Drunk Swedes too Seriously

Invitations to a party or paintball shooting next weekend should not be taken too seriously when the Swede who just got to know you is obviously drunk. They mean well. But don't remind them of the invitation the next day. Instead, let them come back to you to show you they also mean their invitation in their "sober self". In that case, you'll get an invite via text or some other messenger. So don't be disappointed if you don't receive anything. You don't have to save the date in the calendar right away.

## Ignoring

If you see someone on the street who you had a great conversation with, last weekend in the pub, don't expect them to stop and have a conversation with you, not even small talk, or actually, even a simple "hello". Even eye contact is rare if you meet a Swede you have previously met in a drunk state. This doesn't mean that next time you meet the Swede again in the pub he or she won't recognize you. Probably the exact same person comes to you with open arms hugging you, saying, "*Tjjeeeenare! Hur är läget?*".

## Don't drink and drive

*"If you stay sober without having the intention to drive later - you'll be considered 'unnecessarily sober'."*

Swedes are very restrictive when it comes to alcohol and driving. Don't even start calculating "*I'll just have half a glass of wine and I'll be fine.*" Among Swedes, you'd better drink absolutely nothing if you are going to drive your car later that night.

So, dear soon to be Swede, join the queue at *Systembolaget* next Friday afternoon and feel free to get drunk on the weekend - but only then!

# 46. Follow the *Jantelagen*

Often times, when people have very little in the beginning, and suddenly excessive amounts of something special - a lot of success, money or fame - they have the tendency to brag about it. Swedes, on the other hand, remain relatively unnoticed when they achieve something extraordinary. They are less prone to bragging, because they follow the *Jantelagen*, an unwritten law which basically says that "*you are not better than anyone else*".

## Keep Your Feet on the Ground

Well, alright *Jante*, then let's not show off with the new car, house, job, number of record sales or fancy furniture!

For example, just look at Swedish iconic people, like Ingvar Kamprad, the founder of IKEA, who was never seen in a Ferrari or Rolls Royce, kept driving his old Volvo estate for a long time. Or the Members of ABBA, all nice people to talk to, no arrogance. The same goes with high ranked politicians of the country and even most members of the royal family. All friendly people who, despite their achievements or social position, have their feet on the ground and try to not make you feel inferior when you stand opposite them.

So what happens if you show off too much, say, after you received a good grade at school? Well, the people around you might give you slightly jealous, unhappy looks - thinking "*vem tror den där människan han/hon är?!*", "who does he/she think he/she is?!".

For example, if you want to celebrate and outstanding achievement, just make sure you only tell it to those who will not feel too bad about it. Tell it to your cat, *Findus*, for example.

I have met Swedes who regularly got the best grades at school or university, but never told their friends about it. Instead, they preferred to lie and say they just got average grades, fearing others' jealous reactions and even exclusion.

But don't only avoid showing off, it is an equally important part of the *Jantelagen* not to show too much self pity. Don't tell your friends and colleagues how much bad luck you had recently, or how much pain you feel in your knees when you walk up the stairs. Tell them only once. If Swedes want to know more about your health problems, they'll ask you where you get treatment and whether you have already tried to solve it by having an Alvedon.

# Where Does the *Jantelagen* Come from?

The Jantelagen stems from a novel, *En flykting korsar sitt spår* (1933), written in Norwegian, by the Danish author Aksel Sandemose, in which he states the eleven rules from the village of Jante, a fictional place in Denmark which is inspired by Sandemose's hometown, Nykøbing.

## Anti-Jante

Those who like to be a bit rebellious like to call themselves being *anti-jante* or print "f*ck jante" on a t-shirt or write a similar comment on their Instagrams.

Police won't go after you if you break the law of Jante, but major parts of Swedish society might punish you with exclusion, if you overdo it.

Bad news then for everyone who wants to move to Sweden and fancies golden Lamborghinis or long conversations about luxury spa experiences.

So, dear soon to be new Swede, act according to *Jantelagen*! Get a silver Volvo *kombi* and start talking about the ongoing renovation in your cottage house. But only if you do the handicraft yourself! Become a *lagom* Swede!

# 47. Lagom

## What is Lagom?

*Lagom* is the Swedish expression for "in moderation", "just right" or "not too much and not too little", as the Swedes like to answer this question, with their sweet Swedish accent.

They claim, having a word that describes "in moderation" is unique among all languages in the world.

## When to Say Lagom

*Lagom* can mean different things in different contexts.
- Positive: *"lagom varm"*, "perfectly warm".
- Negative: *"lagom kul att jag brutit benen"*, can be translated to "not cool that I broke my leg".
- Ironical: *"han är ju lagom smart"*, meaning "he is not the smartest".

## Where Does Lagom Come from?

Many Swedes believe the myth that the word *lagom* comes from the ancient times when most Swedes were farmers or Vikings and drinking from the same horn or bowl. When they handed it around in circles, they tried to make sure that everyone gets their "fair share" - *laget om*, "around the whole team".

But in reality, the word *lagom* derives from *laghum*, meaning "according to law".

So, dear soon to be Swede, whenever you're asked by other Swedish visitors about the meaning of *lagom*, continue to explain that it originates from that situation where a team of Vikings were sharing one big horn of wine!

# 48. Eat Candy on Saturdays

Sugary food is popular all over the world. Almost everyone loves to eat a piece of chocolate or colorful candy. So do Swedes. They actually have the highest consumption of candy in the World. 17kg, that's the amount of candy (including pastry) you'll have to eat to become like an average Swede.

But most Swedes, particularly the younger ones, are not allowed to eat candy whenever they want. Swedish parents prevent children from eating too much by adapting a rule they themselves learned as children: Sweets (preferably) only on Saturdays!

The concept of eating candy on Saturdays is called *lördagsgodis*, literally "Saturday's candy", and very popular among Swedes.

But before you go to a Swedish supermarket next Saturday, there are a few things you need to know. Here is a list of candy Swedes like to eat, including instructions on how to attain them:

## Weird Swedish Sweets

### Naturgodis

*Naturgodis* are in essence: nuts on the inside and chocolate on the outside. They are usually placed close to the fruit department, to make you believe that you actually choose something healthy from nature. Naturgodis won't help you lose weight, but you'll have a better conscious keeping it.

### Saltlakrits

If you want to punish friends from outside Europe, make them eat *salty licorice*. Many Sweden visitors find it disgusting. Most Swedes like it. I'd say, to become more Swedish, you have to put at least 10% *saltlakrits* in your *godispåse* (candy bag) next Saturday.

## Kex

You probably pronounced it wrong. This with chocolate covered hard waffle, is called Kex, pronounced as "shex".

You have talked to a Swede who claimed, no it's called Kex with a "k"-sound? Maybe you are a Swede yourself and you're convinced it's pronounced that way. Well, you might be right. It's an ongoing discussion in Sweden how to correctly pronounce "Kex". To become more Swedish, you should now pick a side and join the discussion.

## Pingvinstång

A licorice stick with filling. Placed right at the cashier, they are the supermarket's last attack on your "I'm on a diet, so no candy this week"-attempt.

# Get Prepared for Your Candy Consumption

To get your sugar dose, you first have to find the *godisvägg* which is close to the cashier in your local supermarket. *Godisvägg* is the "candy wall". It's usually opposite the "chocolate shelves". Together they form the "sugar canyon". Before that, you'll have to pass deep freezers filled with ice cream. These 15 meters will certainly put your food discipline to a hard test.

So, dear soon to be Swede, start eating candy on Saturdays. Say hello to the *lördagsgodis* routine!

# 49. Take Music and Singing Seriously

As we learned before, people who are bragging with their exceptional skills, are often frowned upon in Sweden. Except when they can sing.

If you are good at singing, you can proudly present your vibrant voice to Swedish ears.

## Talking About Music with Swedes

Things you need to know when you talk to Swedes about singing and music:

- It is *okej* to listen to cheesy pop songs, as long as they are written by a Swede.
- It is *okej* to be a rock musician with all those dark leather clothes, wild hair, makeup and aggressive stage attitude, as long as you are humble and can talk about puppies and flower curtains during interviews.
- You don't have to be good at singing. But let's put it like this, it wouldn't harm your social standing if you are.
- If a Swede says *Nämen gud, jag är så dålig på att sjunga*, "Oh, I sing so badly", and that person really doesn't sing that well, then don't answer "Yeah, I understand now why you were never allowed to join a choir!" (I said exactly that. And I have to admit, the girl didn't find my comment too funny. No idea what she is doing nowadays, but I suspect she's still regularly practicing her vocal skills in her car.)

## Melodic Swedish Language

Why are Swedes so good when it comes to music and singing? Well, I believe their melodic language helps them to find the right tone and be generally more melody-conscious.

Foreigners tend to perceive the way Swedes talk as very pleasant. On first impression, they sound happy and in a good mood. But once you have decoded the nuances of the Swedish language melody, you'll quickly find out that the previously so dearly happy sounding neighbor or shop assistant isn't in such a good mood after all.

## Swedish Singing Passion and Profession

As we found out in a previous step to Swedishness, Swedes usually don't open their mouth a lot, certainly not in conversations. To finally make use of their hidden verbal capabilities, many Swedes decide to join group-meetings where they are directed to synchronously say words in a melodic way. Those groups are called '*kör*', *choirs*. 600.000 Swedes (6% of Sweden's population) have joined one or more.

Since interest in music is wide spread in Sweden, some Swedes have achieved international success as musicians, song writers and singers.

Sweden is not only the home country of popular musicians or bands like ABBA, Roxette, Ace of Base, Avicii or Zara Larsson. Popular songs from stars like Justin Timberlake, Lady Gaga, Backstreet Boys and Celine Dion, have been written and produced by Swedes, too.

*"Sweden is the world's leading exporter of music, in relation to GDP."*

119

For example, *RedOne* (Nadir Khayat) wrote these songs for Lady Gaga: "Just Dance", "Poker Face", "Love Game", "Bad Romance" and "Alejandro".

*Max Martin* (Karl Martin Sandberg) and *Denniz Pop* (Dag Krister Volle) created songs for Britney Spears, Celine Dion, Pitbull, Backstreet Boys, A-ha, NSYNC, Usher, Ace of Base, Pink, Katy Perry and even Bon Jovi.

The Swedes' musical talent and success make their country the third largest producer of pop music - after the US and UK.

Also, Sweden has won the Eurovision Song contest six times 1974, 1984, 1991, 1999, 2012 und 2015. *Bra jobbat, Sverige!* Well done, Sweden!

# Watch these Music Shows on Swedish Television

To understand Swedish singing passion and talent, dear soon to be Swede, you'll have to watch these shows, at least once.

- *Allsång på Skansen*, a sing along TV-show broadcast from the main stage at the open air museum/zoo Skansen in Stockholm. Only a few times during summer.
- *Melodifestivalen* - pre-selection process of the Swedish representative for the Eurovision Song Contest.
- *Idol* - well, the same Idol as in your old country. Except, this Idol brings singers to the front who actually remain in the public eye longer than just a few months.
- *Körslaget* - choirs compete against each other with interpretations of contemporary popular music.
- *Så ska det låta* - a blend of old and young music celebrities unite behind a piano and compete against another group of musicians, singing songs that put you in a good mood.

So, dear soon to be Swede, switch on the TV, launch Spotify or YouTube to listen to your favorite Swedish musicians and start singing!

# 50. Have a Liberal Attitude Towards Sex

There are some stereotypes about Swedes which I would like to refute and some I'd like to confirm.

Rumor has it that "Swedes get naked whenever possible and that they have sex with everyone who can undress within just a few seconds. Is that true?" Let's find out further below...

## Sexually Open-Minded Swedes

One reason why Sweden is perceived as sexually liberal might be the Swedish movies from the 50s and 60s, where in some, bare female breasts were shown. In those days it was unthinkable in many other countries. Popular movies of that time '*Hon dansade en sommar*' or '*Sommaren med Monika*'. (In those titles you notice again, the Swedes' love for the summer season. When else do they get the opportunity to get their clothes off outside without freezing?)

Also, in 1955, Sweden was the first country in the world to introduce mandatory sexual education in primary schools. The goal was to teach pupils at an early age how to protect themselves from unwanted pregnancy.

## Strong and Independent Feminists

You won't find any strip clubs in Sweden or strongly sexualized advertisements or TV-shows depicting naked women in primarily sexual roles. This should not be interpreted as sexual prudery. But rather, the sexualized display of the female body, to solely please male desires, is seen as sexist and anti-feminist by a big part of Swedish society.

Being a feminist is something the majority of the Swedes pride themselves on.

## Stereotypes

A stereotype about Swedish women is that their attitude towards sex can be considered as, erm, "welcoming".

Swedish men on the other hand are often considered as shy. If you watch Swedish men and women in a night club, you might get the impression that this stereotype can be considered as confirmed. But, hey, Swedish men aren't that shy at all, they are simply used to more flirt-active females. So why rush, if the girls are allowed to pick up the guys as well - without being judged as "easy".

## KK

*"If you're single, get yourself a KK - or five."*

*KK* is an acronym for *knull kompis*, which means "f\*ck buddy" or "friend with benefits".

A friend said a while ago, when she found herself to be single after a long term relationship, that her goal was to have at least five *KK*s, at the same time. After asking her for her progress a few weeks later, she replied in a disappointed way that she only got three.

## Nudity

Another stereotype is that Swedes get naked more easily. And indeed, going naked into a sauna or for a swim in a lake isn't unusual in Sweden. Maybe not too common when many people are watching, but not uncommon among friends or when only a few strangers are present.

# "Sex, Tax & Suicide"

In the 60s, American president Eisenhower said Sweden is a country of "free sex, high tax and suicide".

First of all, Swedes aren't as suicidal as many believe. (In the European comparison of suicides per inhabitants, Sweden is listed at rank 15. Only strongly catholic countries have lower rates of suicide. One reason why the rumor of suicidal Swedes has made the round is that it was one of the first countries to create statistics on this matter.)

Secondly, as we found out in a previous chapter on Swedish tax, they are higher, yes, Eisenhower was right, with that point at least.

And then "free sex". Well, if both want it, consensually, and then do it, then in normal cases no one will *swisha pengarna* after the intercourse, will they?

# Sexually Active Swedes

Some say Swedes have a lot of sex. Of course, long cold winters force Swedes to stay inside. Many Swedes live more than a few miles away from a city. So what else can be more entertaining than getting cosy under a blanket in a cold winter night?

The amount of reproductive intercourse reaches its climax on midsummer day (end of June). This is probably the result of stimulation caused by hour long dances around something that represents a phallus, the midsummer pole. This then results in a noticeably higher birthrate nine months later, in the end of March. The most popular date Swedes choose to exit their mother's body and enter the world, nude, is the 22nd of March.

So, dear soon to be Swede, get rid of your shameful associations with sex and start seeing it as a stimulating, pleasurable leisure time activity! Alternatively, as a way to make babies.

# 51. Party Like a Swede

In this chapter, I'd like to focus on the party habits of those Swedes in the typical party age, say between 20 and 35. An age range where most Swedes live in a place they don't have to share with their parents or kids.

## How to Party Like a Swede

Chronologically, follow theses steps:
On a typical Friday evening...

1. Go home from work or studies.
2. Get prepared.
3. Send a message to the pre-party host to check if it's *okej* to bring a friend.
4. Fill a little plastic bottle with the alcoholic drink of your choice. Alternatively, if you are a generous person and want to share your drink with others, take a bag-in-box of wine with you.
5. Carry it in a plastic bag from Systembolaget.
6. Take the bus or go by bike to the pre-party.
7. Enter the place, saying '*Nämen tjeeena!*' to the host, give him or her a short awkward hug.
8. Take off your shoes.
9. Make a round, shake hands with everyone and introduce yourself to those you haven't met yet by simply saying your first name.
10. Immediately forget the names of the people you just met.
11. ... apart from that *snygging* (handsome person) you later want to talk to.
12. Go to the kitchen to put your beer cans or drinks into the fridge.
13. Take one right away to occasionally have a sip out of it.
14. Talk to a random person standing in the kitchen.

15. Ask them from where they know the host.
16. Drink more.
17. Have a seat on the crowded sofa.
18. Talk to the person next to you about what he or she is drinking.
19. Observe how the atmosphere and level of alcohol increases inside of you and others.
20. Let your conversation get interrupted by someone increasing the volume of the music.
21. Feel awkward when that person, who already had a few too many drinks, wants everyone to join for a dance.
22. Raise and move your body in almost rhythmic ways to the sounds of ABBA or Swedish House Mafia.
23. Have another sip to overcome the feeling of awkwardness for a few seconds.
24. Avoid the dance floor in the living room and that shouty sing-along by going to the kitchen for a chat with the other non-screamers.
25. Chat about when to leave to avoid a long queue in front of the pub.
26. Between 22.00 and 00.00 leave the pre-party, after the host stopped the music and shouted '*Nu drar vi!*', '*Now, let's go!*'
27. Before leaving, get stuck in the queue to the toilet that everyone needs to use, except those who spontaneously decide to pee outside behind some bushes or lamp posts.
28. Put on your shoes, notice you collected dust under your sticky socks, which are slightly soaked with beer spill.
29. Walk to the pub/bus station.
30. Speak loudly on the way there.
31. Join the queue to the pub/night club.
32. Get approached/approach strangers and ask them what they are drinking out of their little plastic bottles.
33. Sing a *snapsvisa* (snaps song/drinking song).

34. Get rid of your drink before you are seen by the Security guards (remember, it's mostly not allowed to drink alcohol in public in Sweden).
35. Show your ID at the entrance of the club.
36. Leave your jacket at the coat check (probably the last moment you chatted with the new friends from the pre-party and queue).
37. Join the queue at the toilet before joining the next queue, at the bar.
38. Hit the dance floor.
39. Start flirting (how to flirt in Sweden will be described in a later step).
40. Get seriously drunk.
41. Send *fylle-sms* (drunk texts) to your partner/or friends with benefits, saying you look forward to/would like to see him or her later.
42. If you, as a single, receive an answer, you know you have a backup for the night. If you receive no answer, keep on drunk-dancing or chatting up someone at the bar, asking with sophistication '*Vad dricker du för något?*', 'What are you drinking?'
43. Tell the person you are talking to that you are seriously drunk.
44. Ask '*Where is the after-party?*' if you don't have anyone to spend the night with.
45. Ask '*Wanna have an after-party?*' if you want to spend the night with the person you're talking to.
46. Go home to or with the partner of your choice, if you're not too drunk to do so.
47. But first stop by at a fast food place to get something to eat (or, if you have no one to go to, desperately try to find someone there, who is in the same desperate situation as you are).
48. Go home.

49. Protect! (Just do it! It maybe is hard to remember when you're drunk. But come on, it's better for the both of you. Probably.)
50. Have fun.
51. Wake up with a bad hangover, hoping the other person has left already.
52. Turn your head around noticing you are at that other person's place, and that it's you who hasn't left yet.
53. Go home.
54. Look forward to food and an Alvedon.
55. Get more sleep.
56. Get prepared for a night out on Saturday.
57. Text your friends where to meet for a pre-party.
58. Repeat...

## Some Rules to Remember When You Party in Sweden

- Take your own drinks to pre-parties.
- If you left some drinks or cans of beer at the host's place, make sure to go back to him or her within a week. Otherwise ownership will be transferred to the host - according to unwritten Swedish party law.
- At any party: shake hands with those people you haven't met before, hug those you know. Got used to the risk of ending up in weird half-hug-half-handshake situations.
- Stop offering to invite your friends for rounds at the pub. Because alcohol is expensive in Sweden, no one expects you to invite them, because they don't want you to regret your generosity next time you check your bank account.
- Understand the system of ordering a cocktail or shot at the bar! After ordering *"En Vodka shot, tack!"* you will probably hear the waiter asking you "*Noll-fyra eller noll-*

*sexa?*" a *"Zero point four or zero point six?*", meaning the amount of deciliter of your desired spirit.

- Say "*skål*" a lot! *Skål*, Swedish for *cheers*, is originally an old word for *drinking bowl.*

# How to Act Like a Swede on the Dance Floor

Stop being serious on the dance floor!

If a Swede wants to dance seriously, they join dancing classes, where they receive instructions on how to move rhythmically. Watching Swedes on a dance floor, you will quickly find out that not many have taken any dancing classes.

Nevertheless, it seems to be difficult for Swedes to move their body well, both, when they are either too drunk or too sober. As we learned before - Swedes only achieve that desirable "in-between state of a rush", between 21.00 and 22.00 ("rush hour"), often when they're still at the pre-party.

Dance floors in Sweden can get very bumpy. Don't put on your best shoes. Someone will definitely step on them. If you're lucky, it won't be a high heel of a girl who is trying to pass through the crowd. Get used to elbows hitting your back, waist and head. Don't expect an excuse. If someone turns around and says he or she is sorry, it's probably because that person thinks he or she made you spill your drink - which, of course, in Sweden is much worse than experiencing physical pain.

*"Crossing a Swedish dance floor is a similar experience as a game of American Football, except, in American Football you have a higher chance of making it to the other side without getting bruisers."*

So, dear soon to be Swede, fill your plastic bottle with some liquor blend, join a queue and dance with the Swedes on the dance floor! (No sense of rhythm needed.)

MATTHIAS KAMANN

# 52. Celebrate Swedish Traditions

Swedes don't miss any opportunity to celebrate their traditions. The four most common ones are Easter, midsummer, the crayfish party and Christmas.

## Påsk

When you open your house door and you find Swedish kids standing on your door mat, dressed like witches, don't feel confused that it might already be Halloween. No, it's *påsk*, easter in Sweden.

Those little witches are also on a candy hunt though. So be prepared to have some stocks of candy, to preserve your home from witchcraft. Also, you won't miss if it's going to be *påsk* soon since all shop windows and public flower boxes are decorated with branches full of feathers in flashy neon colors - as bright as those colorful sweat pants, back in the 90's.

## Midsommar

Midsummer always takes place on a Friday, between June 19 and June 25, when Swedes celebrate the longest day of the year. That said, midsummer is not actually in the middle of the summer but right in the beginning. Yeah, this doesn't sound logical, but hey, just have another *snaps* and don't bother arguing about it.

Swedes, just as people in other countries, like to reproduce. And what's great for reproduction? Right. Fertility. Fertility is the core motto of all the midsummer parties in Sweden.

Something Swedes love to tell you, once you let them know that it's your first midsummer in Sweden, is that the *majstång/midsommarstång*, midsummer pole, is actually a phallic symbol. The moment Swedes explain to you they put up a gigantic penis to celebrate fertility is usually the point when the party starts to get really interesting.

Let's sum up a typical midsummer celebration in Sweden: Put on a white dress or one with a flower print, if you're a woman, or a shirt, blue or white, if you're a man. Be outside in a friend's garden, or even better, *sommarstuga*, enjoy the sunshine, set up a white tent and a midsummer pole to dance around later. Line up the party benches and tables. Decorate the table with small Swedish flags or flowers. Have a *smörgåsbord* with *lax* (salmon), *potatis* (potatoes), *sill* (herring), *köttbullar* (meatballs) and for desert *jordgubbar* (strawberries). Drink snaps, sing *snapsvisor* (drinking songs). Play outdoor games like *kubb*. Dance like little frogs around the midsummer pole, singing *kuwakaka kuwakaka kuwakakakakaaa*. (Swedes pretend to do it mainly to entertain their children. But they love it and do it even when there's not a single child around.) Wear a *midsommarkrans* (midsummer wreath) on your head. Enjoy the sunset. Dance. Flirt. Kiss. At last, midsummer is the celebration of fertility, so celebrate it in its most appropriate way.

*"Swedes consider midsummer as a great opportunity to get drunk or pregnant."*

## Special Midsummer Advice

Buy your cider, beer and other alcoholic beverages one day before midsummer. Because that's when the queue is the longest at Systembolaget, and since you're about to become Swedish, standing in line with 50 other Swedes, holding a heavy loaded grey plastic basket with a black handle for about 30 minutes shouldn't bother you at all.

Make sure not to wear too fine shoes. Not only because you'll spend most of the day walking on grass, but also because the person sitting opposite you might reach out for some "under-table-interaction" with your feet.

If you're a woman, and single, collect seven different flowers to put under your pillow before you go to bed. It's said that in your dream, your future husband will appear.

*"You know you've missed midsummer when more than half of your friends have changed their profile pictures to one showing them wearing a midsummer wreath."*

## Kräftskiva

A long time ago, Swedes who loved to party, found the calm half year between midsummer and Christmas far too long, so they came up with the idea of squeezing in another event in the end of the Summer/early Autumn: *kräftskiva*, the crayfish party. Swedes celebrate the end of the traditional annual ban on fishing for crustaceans, which is between 1st of November and the first Wednesday in August. Since 1994, there is no longer any ban but that's no reason for Swedes to stop this beloved sticky-finger tradition.

It is when Swedes gather – again, in white tents – to eat *kräftor* (crayfish), drink snaps and put on funny hats in the shapes of cones with colorful print. This time, the *smörgåsbord* also consists of bowls of crayfish, often unpeeled.

During a kräftskiva, it is very convenient not to be vegan or vegetarian. You're going to have to do plenty of manual work to get to your food. The *kräftor* have to be peeled off. Then the *bajsrand* has to be removed, which basically is the intestine of the crayfish. (Friendly Swedes will tell you to remove the *bajsrand*. When I joined my first *kräftskiva*, those Swedes around me, who introduced me to procedure of preparing *kräftor*, unfortunately, were not that friendly.)

Before eating it, suck the salty juice (and soul) out of the *kräfta*. Don't forget to use plenty of napkins, to remove the smelly liquid from your hands and shirt. After three or four crayfish, you will probably consider eating more potatoes more appealing, because you either got fed up with the salty taste or the extensive peeling process for a tiny little snack.

To get rid of the taste, if you happen to not like it, drink more snaps.

The day after a kräftskiva, Swedes tend to feel a bit sick in the stomach, but instead of blaming the countless snaps-shots, they say *"jag tål inte kräftor"*, *"I 'react' to crayfish"*.

## Extra Tip, for any Swedish Party: Know a *Snapsvisa* by Heart

One of the most popular drinking songs in Sweden is '*Helan går*'
And here are the lyrics, which you should learn by heart:

*Helan går*
*Sjung hopp faderallan lallan lej*
*Helan går*
*Sjung hopp faderallan lej*
*Och den som inte helan tar*
*Han heller inte halvan får*
*Helan går*
*(Drink)*
*Sjung hopp faderallan lej*

## Translation

*The whole one goes down*
*Sing "hup fol-de-rol la la la la"*
*The whole one goes down*
*Sing "hup fol-de-rol la la"*
*And he who doesn't take the whole*
*Doesn't get the half one either*
*The whole one goes down*
*[drink]*
*Sing "hup fol-de-rol la la"*

## Jul

Christmas in Sweden is just like Christmas in your old country. Except, there are a few things that might be a little different ... In Sweden...

... on the 10th of December you can watch Swedes lining up in front of churches to watch girls wearing white robes, singing, while holding candles in their hands. One of the girls wears a crown with candles on her head. She plays *Santa Lucia*, the Italian saint of light. Many young Swedish girls wish to become Santa Lucia one day, until they find out that it can be very difficult to remove the dripped wax from the hair and scalp.

... you drink a mulled wine with fragrant spices called *glögg*, to which you add almond slices and raisins, which you later fish for with a little spoon and lots of patience.

... you celebrate Christmas on Christmas eve, the 24th of December.

... you eat Swedish Christmas food: for once you don't just have another *smörgåsbord*, no, that would be a little boring after having had one for *påsk*, *midsommar* and the *kräftskiva* already. Now you have a *julbord* (christmas table) instead. And, as you can imagine, it's contains pretty much exactly the same ingredients as a normal *smörgåsbord*, except now you also put some *glögg*, *julskinka* (Christmas ham) and candles on the table as well.

... after the first round of heavy eating, you gather with the other family members in front of the TV to watch *Kalle Anka* (Swedish for *Donald Duck*). Yes, all grownups watch Kalle Anka, too, not just the children. And they watch it every year. Don't expect a TV broadcast of new episodes every year. No, they show the almost same collection of clips every time. After a couple of years in Sweden, you will know each line or sound that *Musse Pigg* (Mickey Mouse) and *Långben* (Goofy) say to each other on their hilarious camper-journey through the mountains. Whether you like it or not.

... while watching TV you'll probably also have a plate covered with cookies standing in front of you on the living room table. Those cookies are very likely in the shape of a blossom or heart, called *pepparkakor*, gingerbread. Pepparkakor have been popular in Sweden since the 14th century. As a new-Swede, you should get excited over a *pepparkaka* that breaks into exactly three pieces when you push it with one finger into your other hand palm. It's said it brings you luck.

... if you didn't find yourself lucky with the *pepparkakor*, wait for another Swedish Christmas tradition: Swedes put an almond into the *risgrynsgröt* (rice pudding). According to Swedes, the one who gets it served will either get married next year or simply have luck. One option doesn't always necessarily exclude the other.

So, dear soon to be Swede, go to Systembolaget in time and join a traditional Swedish celebration!

# 53. Avoid Conflicts, Be Neutral (And a bit Shy)

Anyone who says Swedes lack passion is wrong. Swedes just concentrate it in very specific areas, like drinking games, midsummer celebrations, eating kebab-pizza and minimalistic home decoration.

Yes, Swedes may appear to be shy. Whether in the subway or bus, in Sweden you will notice it's rare that two unfamiliar Swedes choose to sit next to each other as long as at least one double seat is unoccupied.

Swedes really don't like to be close to strangers or even have eye-contact with them, certainly not on their way to work. This is just one example of when Swedes may seem to be distant or even antisocial.

## Individualism

But don't mistake this behavior as impoliteness. What can be perceived as coldness, is oftentimes just a way Swedes behave when they don't want to bother others. '*I don't want to interfere with your stuff. And I will take care of my own.*'

Swedes take care of their own agenda. They don't want others to comment on it. They will also not comment on yours.

## Conflict Avoidance

The most intense way of conflict is war, right?

As we learned in a previous chapter, Sweden has been a war-free country since 1814, over 200 years. Pretty cool, heh.

Swedes hate war so much, they even send some of their own people to other conflicting countries to convince them about the benefits of not being at war. Those diplomats have reached international success and recognition. And when you speak with Swedes about politics (which is unlikely to happen, unless you're a politician) you will see a shine in their eyes when you mention names like *Dag Hammarsköld* or ... , well, I haven't talked that much about politics since I moved to Sweden either, if I'm honest.

## Neutrality

A way for Sweden to stay out of conflict has been for many years to remain *alliansfri*, free from alliances. Sweden is not even in the NATO.

They also considered an investment into a strong defense unnecessary. "Why arms if there's no one to shoot at?"

Now, that the political world climate has gotten a bit rougher, Swedes decided it might be good to join the side that appears to be stronger - it's a political path Sweden already successfully went on in the past.

This is their interpretation of *alliansfrihet*, and it already worked in the beginning of the 2nd world war, when Germany was busy invading most of its surrounding countries. Back then, Sweden made a pact with Nazi Germany, saying, *'Please don't invade us! You can even use our railways if you want to, okej?'* Back in the days, Germans didn't fancy excessive amounts of wood or outdoor camping (yet), so they were satisfied with the railway option. Being able to pass Sweden by train seemed convenient for all German soldiers who otherwise would have gotten seasick on the ferry to oil-rich Norway.

Although Swedes have been strictly sticking to their "free from alliances" policy, political discussions about joining NATO arise as regular as foreign military airplanes intrude Swedish airspace or submarines pop up in Stockholm's archipelago.

## Conflict Avoiding Swedish Friends

On a personal level, you will also have to get used to conflict avoiding and consensus seeking Swedish friends. Whereas your old friends back home will probably tell you when you're doing something wrong, your new Swedish friends rather remain silent and avoid any uncomfortable dispute until the problem goes away by itself.

Swedes try to avoid expressing conflicting opinions. When Swedes are angry, you will hardly recognize it in the beginning. They make almost exactly the same facial expression when they are in an angry mood as when they've just won the lottery.

When they feel they have to express something that could be perceived as conflicting, they skilfully wrap it in soft words and phrases. For example, if you have to agree on a common side dish together, you might say '*I want potatoes*'. After you have said that, a Swede who might hate potatoes but wants rice instead might likely reply with: '*Jag skulle kunna tänka mig att det hade varit trevligt om vi provade något nytt istället, som ris till exempel. Vad tycker du?*', 'I can imagine that it would have been nice, if we tried something new instead, like rice for example. What do you think?', which is the Swedish version of: 'I prefer rice.'

Shouting Swedes are rarely heard in public as well. Pass by a construction sight or walk through the main shopping street of any Swedish city. No one screams or shouts. To hear them raise their voices, you have to go to a football match or noisy nightclub.

## Spontaneous Visits from Swedes? Unlikely!

Don't be spontaneous: Never just go to your neighbor, even if he or she is a close friend, without calling or booking a time in advance. Again, this seems shy and cold. But they really just don't want to be disturbed or disturb you when you're doing your thing. Whatever that thing is.

So, dear soon to be Swede, join this individualistic society, embrace individualism and don't visit your friends unannounced!

# 54. Take Your Work Seriously

Apart from weekends, holidays and sick leave days, Swedes go to work. When you go to a normal Swedish workplace, you might find out that things work a bit different than in your old country.

Here are a couple of things to remember, in case you ever fancy working in a Swedish company or cooperate with Swedes:

Dress casually at work. Unless you're maybe a nurse or soldier.

Be punctual. That means, make sure you come to work in time, and leave work on time as well. When you have an appointment for a meeting at work at 10.00, it's better to be there a few minutes early than only one minute too late. If you happen to come too late, the whole group will punish you with very subtle annoyed looks, telling you that you messed up.

Most bosses won't expect you to work overtime. Overtime is uncommon among most office jobs, unless a big project is on the table, of course. But otherwise, work exactly those hours you're supposed to. Working extra, very often, to impress your boss, will only show him or her that you can't manage your workload very well. It also increases the risk that you could burn out, have more days of sick leave and feel overall less satisfied at your current workplace. Most Swedish work places want you to feel good and won't squeeze the last drop of working power out of you.

Work hard, but try to "*stressa inte för mycket*", don't stress too much.

If you discover some incorrect behavior among your colleagues, make sure to report it to your closest workplace friend to *skvallra om det*, gossip about it. But definitely not to your boss (who actually would be able to improve the situation). You don't want a conflict, do you?

According to law you have yearly (at least) 25 days of holidays at your disposal. Most of which you will probably take during the months of July.

You're entitled to 480 days of paternity leave. 90 of those days are reserved for the dad. Around 25% of the paternity leave is taken by fathers.

Expect the company to pay for trips to kick-off events and trade shows, where your Swedish colleagues are likely to indulge in ample eating and drinking. The bonding process may be taken a bit too seriously and moved as far as to the hotel bed.

When you make an appointment in, say, a couple of months, get used to saying the week number first: *'Nästa mote - vad sägs om vecka 35?'* *'Tyvärr, då är jag på Kreta med min sambo. Men vecka 37 skulle passar utmärkt.'* 'Next meeting - what about week 35?', 'Unfortunately, I'll be in Crete then. But week 37 would fit perfectly.'

It's rare Swedes blend work contacts with private friends. The first time your working colleagues meet your friends will probably be on your own wedding or funeral.

Share your ideas with your boss about how you would change something at work. He or she will appreciate your attempts (even if not followed up) and give you the feeling that you actually have an impact on the decision making process.

When you hand in your CV to apply for a job, don't waste time on collecting and attaching old documents. A few phone numbers to previous employers are enough. What your new boss or human resource personnel likely will do, is call your previous employers to have a chat about your working performance at McKinsey and McDonalds. This is often considered more important than the grades on a graduation certificate from Oxford or Uppsala University.

So, dear soon to be Swede, hand in your CV to a Swedish company and get used to greeting your boss with *God morgon, Bengt!* (Good morning, Bengt!) or *Hej Ann-Marie!* (Hello Ann-Marie!) when you enter the office, while wearing a polo shirt or pullover!

# 55. Enjoy Typical Swedish Food

There is some food in Sweden you should definitely try because it's really delicious. Then there is Swedish food which is rather disgusting but you should try anyways because you want to join the conversation about how bad it really is, like for example *surströmming* or *blodpudding*, blood pudding.

## Food You Find in Almost Every Swedish Kitchen Cabinet or Refrigerator

### *Knäckebröd*, Hard Bread

Of course you have heard about Swedish *knäckebröd*, hard bread. You maybe even have a package of *knäckebröd* in your kitchen cabinet. Swedes love it. 85% of Swedes have *knäckebröd* at home.

In the old days it was very important to store food for a longer time, which is why a lot of food was dried or smoked. To become more Swedish, you have to learn to appreciate this crumbling bread and accept the pain of a cut open roof of the mouth and plenty of crumbs spread around your table and kitchen floor.

### *Saltat Smör*, Salty Butter

Swedes eat a lot of salty stuff. Butter is one of the foods they like to taste salty. You can buy *osaltat smör*, unsalted butter, but most Swedes use the salted one to spread on their bread with a handy wooden *smörkniv*, butter knife.

## Kalles Kaviar

Yes, it's caviar but far not as fancy as it might sound. Classic *Kalles Kaviar*, is just a mix of cod or pollock spawn blended with sugar, salt, potato flakes and tomato puree.

Something your Swedish friends probably did not know yet: the iconic blond kid on the blue tube is the son of the managing director at the time of the product launch, back in 1954.

# Typical Swedish *Husmanskost*

(Literally: house man fare)
Here are a few much common dishes you might get served in a restaurant if you ask for something typically Swedish:

- *Köttbullar*, meatballs.
- *Pyttipanna*, or *pytt i panna*, meaning 'small pieces in a pan'. Little cubes of potatoes, onions and any kind of chopped meat, which is fried in a pan together with egg or pickled beetroot. It was originally made as a dish with leftovers.
- *Janssons Frestelse*, 'Jansson's temptation', a casserole made of potatoes, onions, pickled sprats, bread crumbs and cream.
- *Smörgåstårta*, 'sandwich cake'. When Swede once told me they are going to eat *smögåstårta* as a main dish, I was a bit surprised at first, because I expected to have to eat a sweet cake. What I instead received was a cold cake made of several layers of white rye bread with creamy fillings in between. The base usually is mayonnaise and eggs. Add some shrimps, ham, cucumbers, tomatoes and on top sliced lemons and you'll have a classic looking *smörgåstårta* to serve for your next birthday in Sweden.

But, of course, as a real Swede, you'll not only eat typically Swedish food but also delicacies from other countries as well.

Preferably pizza, fries, kebab (sometimes even a combination of all the aforementioned), Asian food and of course hamburgers.

## Swedish Cakes and Pastry

When you meet a Swede for a fika (coffee break), you will probably find yourself eating one of the following pastries:

- *Kanelbullar*, cinnamon buns/rolls. Swedes are so obsessed with them, they even celebrate their existence, every year on the 4th October: *kanelbullens dag*, day of the cinnamon buns.
- *Chokladbollar*, chocolate balls. Their main ingredients are oatmeal, sugar, coffee, cocoa and butter. You might want to ask an old-Swede how they have been commonly called several years ago... a name that is now politically incorrect.
- *Dammsugare*, or *punschrulle,* 'vacuum cleaner'. Green marzipan on a small cylindrical pastry, the ends covered with chocolate.
- *Prinsesstårta*, princess cake. Even more green marzipan. But now on a cream filled layer cake also consisting of airy sponge cake, and a thick domed layer of whipped cream.


So, dear soon to be Swede, get your *smörkniv*, salted butter and ingredients for *kanelbullar* from the local ICA, Willys or COOP (widespread supermarket chains) and start preparing Swedish food!

# Bonus Step: Flirt Like a Swede

Swedes live in a culture, where, before marriage or even sexual intercourse, the two prospects ideally conduct certain interactions in order to display and assess one another's mate- or date-ability. This process is internationally known as flirting. And here's how the Swedes do it:

## How Swedes Flirt

Ways of how Swedes flirt can be various. To increase the chance of being able to observe flirting Swedes, one should to go to a party, pub or night club. Basically meaning any occasion where Swedes are likely to drink some beverages. To make flirting less awkward Swedes prefer doing it during '*tipsy-time*'.

## Daytime Flirting

Of course, Swedes can flirt even during the day, at work or in the supermarket. But it is rather uncommon, and if it happens it is hardly noticeable for the foreigners' eyes.

Daytime flirting in Sweden can be spotted when you hear one of the flirting individuals finishing the conversation with '*Vi kanske kan ses över en fika någon gång?*', 'Maybe we can meet for a coffee sometime?'

## Party Flirting

There are several scenarios of Swedish flirting to remember, in case you find yourself getting approached by or tried to get hit on by a Swede.

Starting at the preparty, as we learned in a previous chapter, Swedes like to meet up before they go out to the pub or night club. This is very convenient, if you want to make new friends or meet your future love. The advantage: as you enter, you introduce yourself and preselect any potential pursuit for later at the pub.

At the pub, you and often the whole group rarely dance or drink altogether. Hanging out in smaller clusters is more common. It's a great opportunity for you to continue the interaction with that sweet Swedish girl/guy you had this lively conversation about cultural differences, back, when you were standing in the kitchen at the pre-party. Now, at the bar, while waiting to order the next shot or cider you have a great chance to go into depth. But don't just talk, you not only should show your verbal skills, but also display your physical vitality, on the dancefloor, moving to the beats of Avicii's 'Levels' or wave your hands in the air to Håkan Hellström's 'Det Kommer Aldrig Va Över För Mig'. It's time to get closer.

## At the Actual Party

In the meantime, you might notice Swedes using their phone regularly and extensively. Sending 'snaps' (the images, not the drinks) and text messages to their friends in the beginning of the evening. Then, later, Swedes who have the intention to get cozy with someone who they already have gotten to know on previous occasions, reach out to check for a night together. The most common text message sent in Sweden on a Friday/Saturday night between 23.00 - 03.00 in Sweden is most likely "Ses ikväll?" or, to start the request with a little more grace, "Hur är det med dig?", "How are you doing?".

# If Nothing Worked out, 'Kvart i Två Ragg'

In case the pub is about to close and you're still standing with a bored friend and a half empty bottle of beer on the side of the dance floor, make a few steps forward.

Hope for a '*kvart i två ragg*', 'quarter to two flirt/hook up' - out of desperation since you haven't been lucky so far and your *KK* hasn't replied yet. Face it, you're drunk, can hardly say a complete sentence or even walk straight anymore. Never mind all the other 'evening leftovers' are exactly in the same kind of condition. So make sure to get close to one of them as long as the music is playing (no need to talk) and as long as the bright lights are still off (easier not to reveal your drunk facial expressions).

While standing in the diffuse light, you might notice someone coming up to you to perform a dance-like move to catch your attention or just bump into your behind with their behind from behind. That's about it, before you can react you might find yourself kissing the person in the middle of an emptying dance floor. You probably just scored a person that you in the beginning of the evening commented on as "*funkar i krig*", "is ok during war time".

After a spontaneous decision to keep your eyes open while kissing, in favor of not loosing the balance, you put a lot of focus on actually hitting your short-term partner's lips or tilting your head in order to remove a wet tongue from penetrating your ear.

As one of you starts reaching for the belt of the other, it's probably time to join the queue to the coat check and find a place somewhere else to continue the exchange of passion and *Billy's pizza*.

# Sunday Stroll

If you are fed up with nightly encounters and sexual adventures, and instead aim for a deeper long term relationship, ask for a *söndagspromenad*. This means, you have an actual interest in the person. Combined with several *fikas*, it means 'serious business'. That's how long-term relationship-material is tested in Sweden.

## Movie Nights

If you invite a Swede over to your place for a *fika*, as the first date, he or she will assume that you probably want sex. Swedes will be absolutely sure you want sex, if you invite them for a movie night. "*Ska vi kolla på en film tillsammans?*", "Shall we watch a movie together?", is so overused in situations where someone actually wants to explore someone else's body, that it won't be taken seriously any longer. Sorry for you if you really just want to watch a movie with someone. It's simply not possible to express such an invitation without creating wrong expectations. "*Men jag vill verkligen bara titta på en film, inget annat!*" "But I really just want to watch a movie, nothing else!" - Yeah, of coooourse...

## How Swedish Men Flirt

A couple of my female friends confirmed: Swedish men's flirting cues are a bit more subtle than in other countries. For example, they won't stare at you or even try to say more than a few sentences. Basically you can divide Swedish male flirting activities into two categories:

1.  Standing in one spot, looking nice and groomed. Waiting for a Swedish girl to come over, while having a drink - among Swedish men, this seems to be already considered a flirting attempt.

2. Being drunk, dancing on the dance floor, close to a girl, slightly touching her waist or back, checking her reaction and waiting for her to do the next step. If there's no recognizable success within 30 seconds, they are on to the next. Simple. No fuzzing around.

## How Swedish Women Flirt

The way Swedish women flirt can be described in the following steps:

1. They take what they want.

So, if you're a man, get used to a comparably aggressive flirting behavior of Swedish girls.

If you're a woman and you had to be afraid of being called a slut whenever you would flirt with more than one man within 30 minutes, back in your old country, good news: Welcome to Sweden, where you're free to approach the guy you fancy and increase your mating frequency - without being judged as "loose". You're just a sexually liberated woman. No need to be ashamed over satisfying your natural needs and desires. Whatever those might be.

## Levels of Relationships in Sweden

Levels of Swedish relationship status might come as a shock to you, if you have been living in a society where you are either "single" or "in a relationship with someone". In other words, you either have a boyfriend/girlfriend or not.

Now, in Sweden, it's getting a little more complicated than that. As we learned before, Swedes are a little more individualistic and want to live independently as long as possible. To guarantee a smoother transition from single life to a more stable long-term relationship, they have established in between steps, which make it easier to get over their fear of commitment.

## Level 1: Seeing Someone

You just saw someone some time, for a date or two. But you're not exactly sure whether you really have an interest in that person yet.

## Level 2: Dating

You dated a person several times and believe you have feelings for the other person. Potential partnership prospect.

## Level 3: Exclusively Dating

Now, you really have feelings for each other and say that you won't mess around with others anymore.

## Level 4: Unofficially Together

You two are in a relationship, maybe your closest friends know, but still, you want to wait whether the bond is strong enough, because you don't want to embarrass yourself, in case one breaks up after a while.

## Level 5: Officially together

Time to update your social media profile and let your parents know that you'd like to introduce someone at the next family gathering. Serious stuff.

## Level 6: Sambo

You have decided to live in the same apartment. (*Sambo* stands for '*samboende*', meaning 'living together' or 'cohabitation'.) Having moved in with a Swede means that within less than a year, one of you will either break up, get pregnant or decide that it might be better to continue the relationship as '*särbo*', living apart together.

## Level 7: being 'gift'

'*Gift*' means 'married'. The same word also means 'poison'. No wonder why an increasing number of Swedes decides to remain in a *sambo-relationship* rather than getting poisoned.

# Extra level: *KK*

And, as previously mentioned, the '*KK-relationship*', 'friends with benefits'. Not rarely this kind of liason outlasts the length of a typical Swedish love relationship by some margin.

So, dear soon to be Swede, adjust to Swedish dating and mating habits and find your future long-/short-term partner in Sweden!

# Thank You for Reading "How to be Swedish"

Now that you know how to eat, dance, celebrate, drink and love like a Swede, go out and put your new skills into action! Invite someone for a *fika* or a *söndagspromenad*...

You can always go back to this book and check whether you still follow these *steps to Swedishness* correctly. Or why not use this book to start a conversation with a Swede, asking whether he or she agrees to these steps.

If you liked the book and feel you already have achieved a high level of *Swedishness*, consider giving this guide to a good friend who you think might need it, and attach a handwritten note with a friendly message to it.

If you didn't like the book, give it to a friend that you don't like and don't add a written note. (Sorry, if you read this after someone gave it to you without that note.)

# More About Sweden

I really hope you enjoyed reading this book. To learn more about Sweden, Swedish experiences or quirks (or me) visit my blog:

www.HejSweden.com/en/

More about this book, personal recommendations or useful information how to get prepared for a trip to or life in Sweden, visit:

www.HowtobeSwedish.com

# Thank You Sweden

When I came to Sweden, back in 2005, for a semester abroad, I expected to spend a few months in a country with sunny summer nights, cold winters, vast forests, beautiful blondes, lovely lakes and Ikea in every city. As it turned out, I was wrong with the Ikea expectation - only.

Sweden is a wonderful place! Of course, living in Sweden isn't always easy (adjusting to a new culture, understanding how society works or learning a new language can be hard), but I always felt welcome in Sweden.

Honesty, equality and harmony are values that come into my mind when I think about Sweden. Desirable values, lived by wonderful people, in a beautiful environment.

I want to say *"Thank you!"*, to all Swedish people, for welcoming me with open arms and for giving me the opportunity to create the life I aspire, in this truly great country.

Thank you, Linnaeus University/Växjö Campus, for an education and a student life that I never could have imagined, not in my wildest dreams.

Thank you, Sweden!

*Tack, Sverige!*

Matthias Kamann
January 2017, Växjö, Sweden

MATTHIAS KAMANN

© Matthias Kamann, 2017

Publisher:
Matthias Kamann, Växjö, Sweden

Cover design and illustrations:
Matthias Kamann

1$^{st}$ edition, 2017

ISBN 978  91  983799  0  7

www.HowtobeSwedish.com

www.HejSweden.com

www.MatthiasKamann.com